A rejuvinating Sun Room allows for weather-independent 'outdoor' enjoyment.

Quality in execution and thoughtful detailing is a staple of our products. From homes that have an old-world elegance and charm to homes styled for the contemporary family with progressive needs, Lakeville Homes seeks to meet and exceed expectations with each home. Homes are designed to be lived in and to accommodate life's every day tasks while providing an elegant backdrop for entertaining life's most special occasions.

For every home, we understand that it is not only our reputation, but also our clients' dream on the line. Nevertheless, we look forward to the challenge in surpassing our customers' expectations.

...because Your home is a reflection of you.

LAKEVILLE HOMES
EST. 1985

www.lakevillehomes.com
1824 - 114th Avenue Northeast
Bellevue, Washington 98004
425.453.8388

Seattle's Premier Home Builder...

...making your home a reflection of you...

Lakeville Homes was conceived in 1985 from a vision of creating exceptional homes that reflect the owners' lifestyle and accomplishments. With our clients' goals constantly in mind, we develop all of our homes under the model of combining detailed planning, superlative design, excellent communication and management skills.

Since the outset of Lakeville Homes, we have pursued our vision with vigor and executed our homebuilding model with success. Lakeville Homes has not only produced many satisfied clients, we have also garnered industry recognition for our dedication to excellence.

Nestled on a lush 3-acres in Bellevue, the majestic estate offers sweeping views of Lake Sammamish and epitomizes luxury living.

Refined living is made simple in elegant living spaces created through a collaborative effort between architect, client and home builder.

ARCHITECT: Freiheit & Ho Architects, Inc., P.S.
Bellevue, Washington

BUILDER: Lakeville Homes
Bellevue, Washington

photographs by Randy Corcoran

LAKEVILLE HOMES
EST. 1985

ABOVE: A graceful entrance greets your guests and introduces them to finer living from their first impression.

RIGHT: A picture window frames the stunning view of Lake Sammamish, while the wood detailing provides a sense of grace and majesty.

BELOW: A logical configuration and location makes this contemporary kitchen a centerpiece for the house, as well as the home's social hub.

Unique Homes of the
Pacific Northwest

PUBLISHED BY RHINOBOOKS • BOISE, IDAHO

ART DIRECTION AND DESIGN BY ANITA QUICK

Principal photography by Michael Mathers, Quicksilver Studios, Insight Photography International, Roger Wade and Tim Brown

Additional photography by Steve Young, David Stoecklein, Mark Mularz, Alonso Rochin, Phil McClain, Kirk Keough, Fred Lindholm, Tim Rider, Alan Weintraub, Mark Lisk, Steve Bly, Kevin Syms, Adam Bacher, Holly Stickley, and Strode Eckert Photography, and by the courtesy of the owners of the unique homes featured in this book.

powered by RHINO

OREGON   IDAHO   MONTANA   BRITISH COLUMBIA   WASHINGTON   OREGON   IDAHO   MONTANA   BRITISH COLUMBL

Unique Homes of the
Pacific Northwest

Published by Rhinobooks, LLC
P.O. Box 16348, Boise, ID 83715
www.rhinobooks.net

powered by RHINO

Printed by C & C Offset / China
Editorial Assistance: Bob Struble, Maureen Halloran/Calliope
Cover and book jacket design: Anita Quick

The Publisher would like to thank the various photographers, architects, builders, home owners, realtors and others whose information and images appear in this publication. I would especially like to say thanks to Tim Boyle and Dan & Rory Clark for their invaluable support, as well as my father, Bud Wilks, who by his example taught me persistence and integrity will always prevail.

Thanks to all!
Ron Wilks

Within these pages you will explore the intimate details of some of the most creative, spectacular and unique homes available anywhere in the world. The homes are creative masterpieces that have evolved from the minds of the most prestigious architects, builders and interior designers in the industry. These pictorials provide a personal glimpse into grandiose and spectacular mansions and estates that are of an impressive world-class category. You will also see some of the most unique homes imaginable: Tree Houses, Boat Houses, Cottages, Yachts and structures beyond your wildest imagination. This collection of Pacific Northwest homes is truly remarkable.

I have been blessed with the pleasurable task of investigating the remote regions of the United States to find these residential gems and provide them for your viewing pleasure. So please, sit back, get comfortable and enjoy the impressive works of a very elite class of talented individuals.

Ron Wilks, Publisher
RHINOBOOKS, LLC

Unique Homes of the Pacific Northwest includes some of the most intriguing homes found in Washington, Oregon, Idaho, Montana, and British Columbia.

The homes in this book have been organized by region for your viewing pleasure. A Craftsmen an Design Credits section has been provided in the back of the book that identifies many of the artists and craftsmen that are responsible for creating these spectacular homes. The homes within are creative works of art that define the very essence of the designers, builders and home owners themselves.

Washington
homes
Pages 6-71

Washington

Oregon
homes
pages 72-121

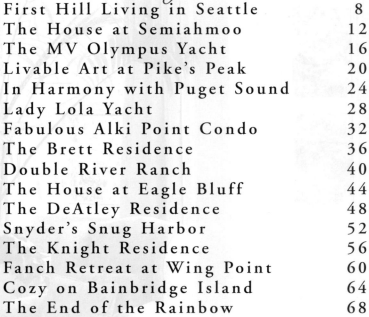

Oregon

Idaho
homes
pages 122-169

Unique

Idaho

Montana
homes
pages
170-181

Montana

British Columbia

British Columbia
Canada homes
pages 182-203

Craftsmen and Designer Credits

A collection of Washington's most original and distinctive homes.

UNIQUE HOMES OF

shington

NORTHERN
First Hill Living in Seattle, The House at Semiahmoo, The MV Olympus Yacht, Livable Art at Pike's Peak, In Harmony with Puget Sound, Lady Lola Yacht, Fabulous Alki Point Condo

EASTERN
The Brett Residence, Double River Ranch, The House at Eagle Bluff

SOUTHERN
The DeAtley Residence, Snyder's Snug Harbor

WESTERN
Knight Residence, Fanch Retreat at Wing Point, Cozy on Bainbridge Island, The End of the Rainbow

The Evergreen State is one of the most diverse areas the United States has to offer. In a single day one can experience majestic mountains, dense rain forests, desert vistas, volcanic splendor, fertile fields of fruits and flowers, an inland sea, a maze of island wonderlands, coastal beaches, and the largest metropolitan area in the Northwestern United States.

Within these wonderfully diverse locations exist some of the most unique homes found anywhere in the world; homes that are as varied as the settings they are found in. In this section of the book you will see both the mesmerizing views of the exterior architecture and locations themselves, as well as the unbelievable beauty and exquisite individualism of their interior spaces, including homes in excess of 27,000 square feet, mansions, high-rise condominiums, beach cottages, and even yachts.

Regions

First Hill Living
in Seattle

Photography by Michael Mathers

First Hill has the distinction of being Seattle's oldest residential neighborhood. First Hill Plaza is considered one of the most prestigious condominium properties in Seattle. Truly in-city living at its finest. The views from this 28th floor home are as spectacular as they come. Sweeping vistas of the city scape, Puget Sound, Lake Union, the Olympic and Cascade Mountains, and fabulous Mt. Baker make the glow of day or the twinkling of evening lights even more amazing.

ARCHITECT: SANDLER ARCHITECTS – SEATTLE, WA
BUILDER: JAS DESIGN-BUILD, INC. – SEATTLE, WA
INTERIOR DESIGNER: ELISABETH BEERS – SEATTLE, WA

This three-bedroom, three-bath condominium features beautiful marble, limestone and granite floors, and the most stunning custom cabinet woodwork found anywhere. The patterned Pompeii Sapele dark wood adds an unusual richness to the space and blends well with the abundant light from the high Northeastern exposure.

Tibetan rugs, European artwork, and an exquisite African sculpture showcased on a Philippian Mulava wood roller lends a pleasurable, artistic, and international flair to the main living areas. High-rise living has a style all its own and is unique to each owner's taste. When combined with the condominium's resort style amenities, such as a swimming pool, exercise facilities, entertainment and guest facilities, and 24-hour security, this living style offers all the creature comforts of home as well as the conveniences of city life.

Comfortable surroundings, Tylek paintings, deep rich woods, and fabulous views make this home the ideal environment. Add to this a personal sauna, steam shower, and high-tech entertainment system, and it is difficult to find a reason to want to go elsewhere.

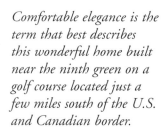

Comfortable elegance is the term that best describes this wonderful home built near the ninth green on a golf course located just a few miles south of the U.S. and Canadian border.

B L A I N E , W A S H I N G T O N

Photography by Michael Mathers

When the owners set out to design their Pacific Northwest dream home, their vision was a home that soaked up the exquisite beauty of towering trees and invited the sun to warm their home and hearts. They wanted a home that truly flowed with the environment. The tall cedars and soaring eagles of Semiahmoo provided the perfect setting.

Having long admired the work of Frank Lloyd Wright, they wanted the outside of the house to bear his trademarks of large overhangs, windows without headers and soffits that flowed into the interior. Lots of light and open spaces were also a priority, as evidenced by ceilings ranging from 10 to 23 feet high.

ARCHITECT: TREVOR EULEY DESIGN STUDIO – VANCOUVER, B.C.
BUILDER: SAND DOLLAR MANAGEMENT COMPANY, – BLAINE, WA

The home exudes the natural beauty of wood and features solid cherry interior doors, custom milled woodwork, and accentuated highlights such as the hand built arch over the entry door shown.

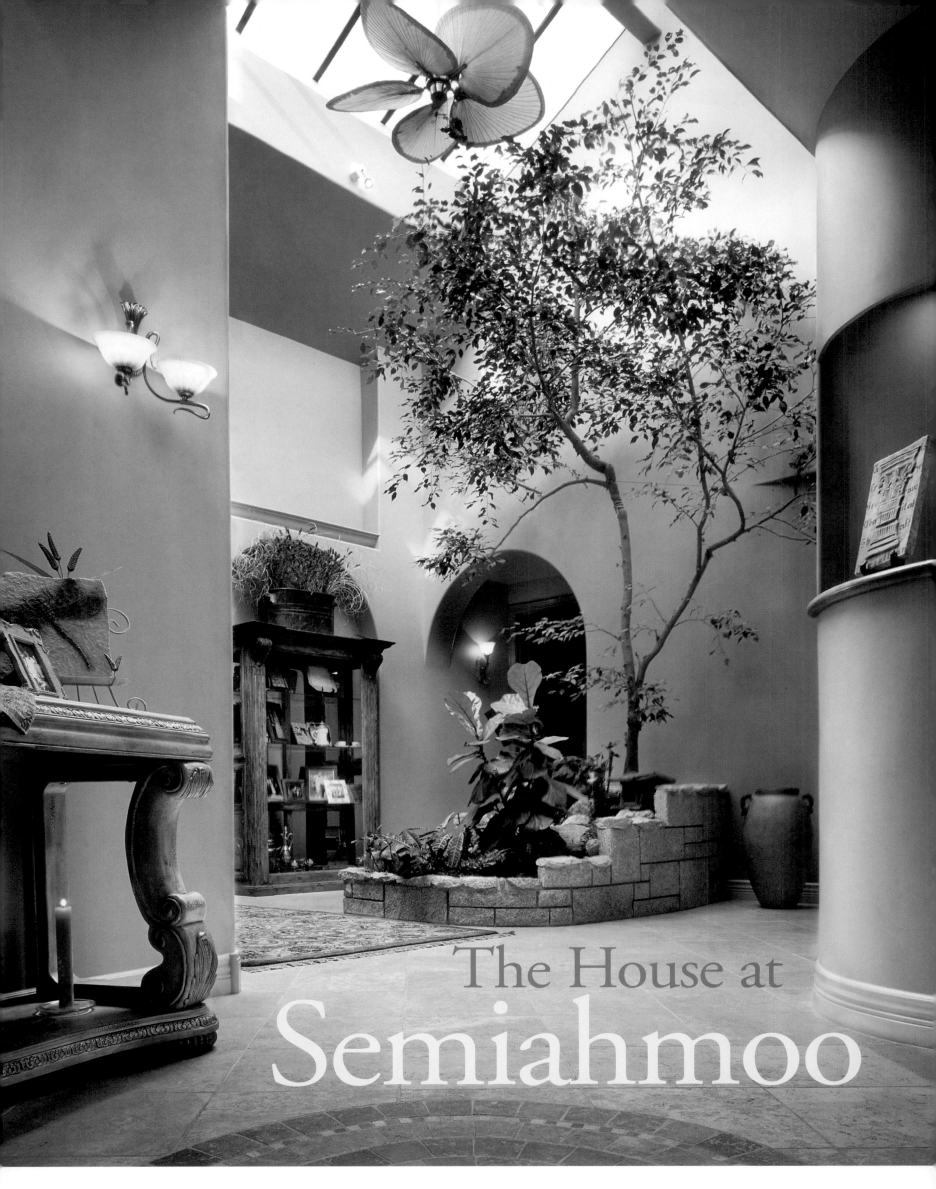

The House at
Semiahmoo

*T*he beautiful kitchen is sized to accommodate large parties. The custom crafted cabinets are furniture grade and the countertops are solid slab granite with double beveled edges. The overall kitchen design is reminiscent of a French country château. Indirect lighting was used above the cabinets to accentuate different levels and heights of cabinetry. The dining room adjoins the kitchen, overlooking the garden and lake and will seat 14 people.

The floors throughout this warm and elegant home are Turkish Travertine with design inserts of tumbled marble.

The custom wooden windows have low E Italian azure blue double window glass to protect the furniture from fading and provide warmth to the sky on cloudy days. Interesting ceiling detail is used to cloak indirect lighting in the main living area.

The master bedroom is a spacious retreat overlooking the lake of the 9th green on the golf course. The ceiling is 10 feet high with indirect lighting concealed in a circular cove.

The Gem of Seattle
The MV Olympus

SEATTLE, WASHINGTON

Photography by Alonso Rochin

This 97 foot, twin diesel, fantail yacht was originally built in 1929 for the president of the New York Stock Exchange. The MV Olympus combines beautiful old world craftsmanship and new world comfort to provide a nostalgic retreat on one of the most elegant yachts remaining from the 1920's era.

The MV Olympus has a rich tradition and history. She has been host to dignitaries and celebrities over the years, ranging from President Truman in her earlier days, to Senator Warren Magnuson, Julie Andrews, Robin Williams, and Governor Gary Locke in more recent times. The yacht even displays the original guest log with President Truman signing his address as "temporarily 1600 Pennsylvania Avenue". The yacht was taken by the U.S. Government during WW II to serve as a navy vessel. After the war, it was purchased as "war surplus" by the State of Washington in the 1940's and refurbished into the "Governor's Yacht". It became a major item of controversy when the public discovered that over $100,000 was spent on refitting her, consequently costing Governor Mon Wallgren his re-election and causing the yacht to be promptly sold by the newly elected Governor.

BUILDER: NEW YORK YACHT, LAUNCH & ENGINE CO. – NEW YORK
OWNERS: DIANE & JOHN VAN DERBEEK – SEATTLE, WA
CAPTAIN: SCOTT GIENOW – SEATTLE, WA

The yacht has been privately owned and operated since 1949. The boat's current owners, John and Diane VanDerbeek, performed a complete interior renovation in 2000, restoring the grand old lady to her original luxury and condition. The boat continues to play a prominent role in the life of the City of Seattle, is often used to lead the yacht parade for the Opening Day of Boating each spring, and also serves on special occasions as the "unofficial" Governor's Yacht.

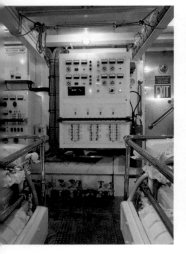

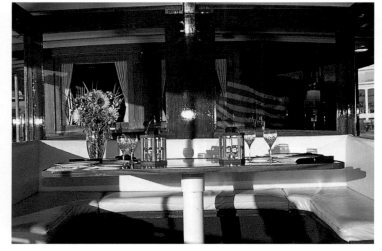

The main salon is elegantly furnished. The formal dining area seats eight, while the fantail can comfortably accommodate twelve for formal luncheons or dinners. The fantail can also be open or closed as desired. Four handsomely decorated staterooms have their own private entry baths. The exquisite use of brass, teak and oak provides all those aboard with an experience that has been described as "gliding along in a stately manner". This yacht is truly a gem and the pride of Seattle.

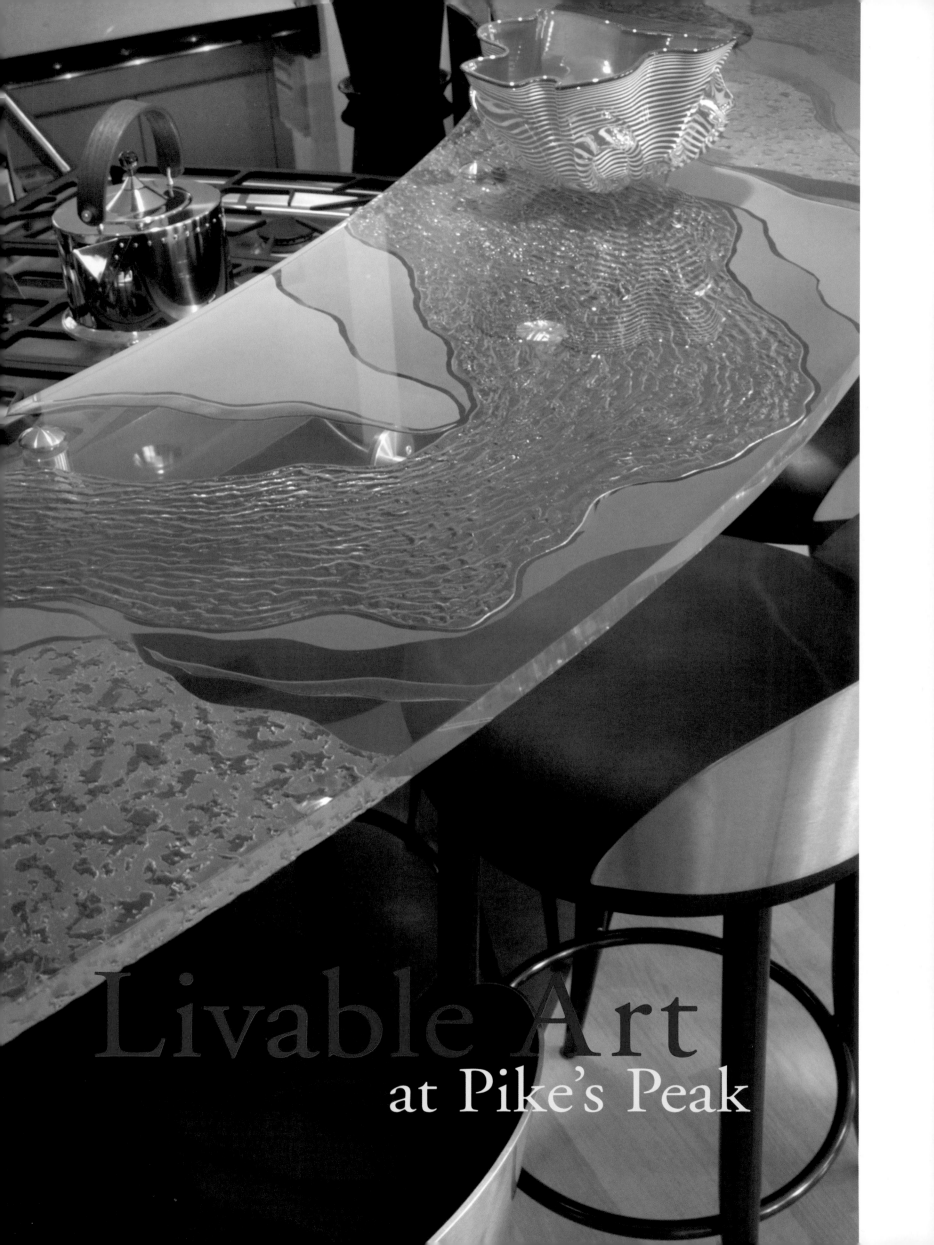

Livable Art
at Pike's Peak

BELLEVUE, WASHINGTON

Photography by Michael Mathers

This custom home is a modern masterpiece wherein the architectural design, modern interior art, beautiful furnishings, and interior design all melt into one. The home is a perfect blend of Art Deco, Mediterranean elegance, and modern design; making it both a home and a work of art. Meticulous attention to detail and creative use of space are prevalent throughout the home.

The unique art coves built into the walls utilize distinctive spot lighting to highlight attractive glass-art and sculptures. The glass-art etched double entry doors lead to a rotunda of elegant columns with curving walls & ceilings in the entry area. This home provides many intriguing designs and styles around every turn.

ARCHITECT: AKHAVAN ARCHITECTURE – LOS GATOS, CA
BUILDER: THOMPSON RESIDENTIAL DEVELOPMENT – BELLEVUE, WA
INTERIOR DESIGNER: SALLY A. THOMPSON – BELLEVUE, WA

Nestled in the private wooded hills of Bellevue, Washington, this 4,420 square foot home has spacious 17 and 12 foot ceilings in key living areas with abundant sunlight throughout. Extensive use of marble, granite, and rich hardwood flooring, along with the custom hand blown glass sinks nestled in granite, surround visitors in beauty wherever they turn. The use of custom glass countertops, shelving and accent pieces, along with curved slab granite in the kitchen and wet bar, present stunning displays of artistry that flow well with the other areas in the home. The 1,800 square feet of granite and marble variations include rare cobalt chip and Brazilian plum, The overall impact of the interior design and decoration is absolutely stunning.

The freeform blend of function and design is evident everywhere in this home. The theme is also prevalent outside with the pool, waterfalls, spa, cabana, raised seating area, built in BBQ, and sports court area. "Livable Art" is a very appropriate description of this classy, tranquil and pleasant environment.

In Harmony
with Puget Sound

MUKILTEO, WASHINGTON

Photography by Michael Mathers

*D*esigned to respect nature and blend with the environment, this astonishing home is the perfect compliment to its surroundings. Designed by Taliesin West Architects, a subsidiary of the Frank Lloyd Wright Foundation, Windintide is one of the few truly environmentally friendly, "green" homes in the state of Washington. It complies with all state energy codes and is the tightest custom-site-built home on local record.

The repeated curved fin design creates a relaxed rhythm and structure for the continuous band of skylights located between the fins. The skylights provide a unique ventilation system to cool the home and also allow for a well-lit, openness to the interior spaces.

ARCHITECT: TALIESIN WEST ARCHITECTS -
STEPHEN NEMTIN, SCOTTSDALE, AZ
BUILDER: SHIREY CONTRACTING -
ISSAQUAH, WA

The round openings and curves are a continuous theme throughout the house, and even appear in the detailing of the artfully designed kitchen cabinets. Opposite page: A large circular bronze sculpture, Solar Wind, is centered in the circular opening of the first fin.

$\mathcal{D}$eep, rich Brazilian cherry flooring helps to emphasize the naturalness and warmth of the home. Great care was taken to ensure the furnishings matched the artistry and natural surroundings. The home instills a sense of peace, beauty and a love of nature.

The deep blue waters of Puget Sound are visible from every room. The cantilevered terrace wraps around both wings of the house to further enhance the fabulous views.

27

Lady Lola

SEATTLE, WASHINGTON

Duane and Lola Hagadone created their idea of the perfect yacht, with all the amenities of home and built for 'around-the-world travel'. The "Lady Lola" is a 68.4 meter, four level, floating marvel that includes one complete upper deck for the owners' personal use, four guest suites, two dining rooms, a captain's suite, 7 crew cabins, a heated swimming pool, two saloons, study, two tender boats with miscellaneous water toys, observation/media lounge, gaming area, bar, Steinway grand piano, lots of sun lounging areas, leading edge technology control room, galley, six machine laundry, and bullet proof glass. The two and a half year project, built by Oceanco under the direction of the Hagadones, produced a very unique residence that cruises at twelve knots, with a range of 4500 nm, to virtually any port in the world.

The highest priority was for an entire upper deck to be devoted to a spacious and comfortable owners' living area with a 180-degree panoramic view. Lola worked closely with the interior designer, Francois Zuretti, to formulate a design masterstroke that combined materials that promote formality and relaxation, as well as brightness and space, yet has the feel of the livable comforts of home. Furnishings, carpeting and white interior all combine with class and solemnity, accented by a magnificent band of dark apple mahogany ringing the lower walls. The warm and subtle texture of Norwegian birch burl round out an absolutely stunning visual effect in every well-proportioned space throughout the yacht.

BUILDER: OCEANCO/2002, MONACO
INTERIOR DESIGNER: ZURETTI INTERIOR DESIGNERS
CAPTAIN: STAN ANTRIM - SAN DIEGO, CALIFORNIA

The custom features of the yacht are too numerous to display them all, but include such unique features as: privacy system for the owners areas, illuminated panels of sculpted glass, marble floored hallways and bathrooms, a mirrored panel that slides seamlessly hides the stairs to the owners' deck, and glass waterfalls.

*W*indows and mirrors are positioned to allow all 12 seated at the dining table to partake of the magnificent ocean views, while a table for two in the owners' area converts to a table for eight from an ingenious overhead drop down mechanism with the flip of a switch. Lady Lola also features a small discreet serving hatch to the owners' area, fitted wardrobes and drawers, custom tailored dressing room with glass fronted drawers, private communications center, and oh so much more. It even includes, amazingly enough, an 18 hole floating golf course (closest to the pin rules and tour specification floating golf balls). Duane and Lola have managed to make the need for land obsolete.

Fabulous
Alki Point
Condo

WEST SEATTLE, WASHINGTON

Photography by Michael Mathers

This Puget Sound hideaway offers a contemporary and casual atmosphere with unique design elements. This residence emphasizes an open floor plan with few physical transitions segmenting this 4,300 square foot, single floor dwelling. The design theme reflects the owners' sophisticated, yet casual lifestyle.

Expansive views of Elliott Bay and the Olympic mountains provide an ever-changing mural for this waterside urban getaway. Within the solid concrete and steel building frame reside the rare finishes, expertly crafted fixtures, and technological surprises of modern architecture at its finest. Imported lava counter tops capture the icy-blue hue of northern alpine lakes and stacked slate cuttings form walls of variegated texture and color. Venetian plaster skims interior vertical surfaces and translucent mosaics shimmer against the water features of the in-home spa. Central to the living space is a rotating 60 inch HDTV plasma monitor with THX surround sound.

ARCHITECT: GGLO – SEATTLE, WA
BUILDER: KREKOW JENNINGS, INC. – SEATTLE, WA

Reflective glass tiles clad the columns that have been encircled by decorative cast glass shelving.

ustom cabinetry of Anigre veneer blends well with islands and counters of vivid turquoise lava stone and black concrete. A rolling dining table with pistachio-tinted sycamore top creates a flexible dining experience and enhances the pleasurable color schemes in the adjoining areas. Floating lit glass ceiling panels by artist Jerry Newcomb create a rich and welcoming entryway.

The curving hallway leading to the spa is flanked by a richly textured stone wall on one side and a beautifully crafted plaster wall on the other.

The bed in the master bedroom sits graciously against a wall of Sapele veneers and hidden storage.

The 4,305 square foot home includes a spa, steam bath and combination gym/guest room, complete with heated floors. The eight foot steel tub with the perfect profile for a reclining occupant is located next to a basalt wall of water that provides a shimmer and relaxing ambiance. Translucent glass walled sinks combined with iridescent mosaic tile and variegated slate to highlight the steam bath area. The selection of materials throughout the home is very rich in texture and color, collectively giving one the feeling of being surrounded by beauty and peaceful serenity.

The Brett Residence

Photography by Michael Mathers

This Spokane area mansion, nearly a century old, has best been described as a "timeless classic". Originally built in 1917 for T.J. Humbird an executive for the Weyerhauser Company, this seven bedroom, seven bath, 20,000 square foot home transcends its years and remains a remarkably livable, contemporary home with a great deal of grace and functionality. In 1937, Mr. and Mrs. George Jewett took possession and owned it until eight years ago, when Bobbie and Kathy Brett became the third owners of this amazingly resilient old mansion. Other than the recent creation of a wine cellar and remodel- ing the kitchen, master bath and servants' quarters, remark- ably few things have been altered in this wonderful home.

The home's history is steeped in elegance and sophistication. The house is the last mansion created in the Pacific Northwest by architect Kirkland Cutter. The exterior is a traditional Tudor Revival, while the interior is a style described as Southern Colonial Revival. The home features large rooms, well-proportioned spaces, French doors, and many leaded windows to ensure lots of light. A feeling of southern comfort is imparted throughout the home. In days of old, the home was run with a full staff of maids, cooks, butlers, and gardeners. The current owners' influence has brought a more family oriented, relaxed style of living. The Bretts, are the owners of the three pri- mary sports teams in Spokane and the sports emphasis is evidenced in the home, although subtle enough to maintain the superb elegance of the original style.

ARCHITECT: ORIGINAL - KIRKLAND CUTTER - SEATTLE, WASHINGTON
BUILDER & REMODEL: PAT JEPPESEN - SPOKANE, WASHINGTON

The home was a model of future technology when built, incorporating such modern conveniences as gas jets in the fireplaces, a gas heated clothes dryer, and even an in-wall vacuum system throughout the home.

Opposite page: From the original 1908 Brunswick bowling alley in the basement to the third floor 200 capacity ballroom, the home is truly a classic. The home has evolved from a formal showplace to a warm and comfortable family style home with a great deal of class and style that maintains the integrity of the original design.

The impeccable landscaping is accredited to the Olmstead brothers, whose accomplishments include such landmarks as Central Park in New York and the grounds of the Boston Commons.

A sports court and natural rock pond with waterfall have been added recently, all of which help to enhance the beauty and enjoyment of the grounds that overlook downtown Spokane, with a northern panoramic view of the valley and Mt. Spokane.

The Double River Ranch Residence

The entry way was designed to mimic the grand lodge at Glacier National Park. It features two cedar trees that have 60-inch bases. The massive hand carved mahogany doors present a truly impressive sight to all who enter.

WALLA WALLA, WASHINGTON

Photography by Roger Wade

This magnificent 13,000 square foot home is located in Walla Walla, Washington, the "Napa Valley" of the Pacific Northwest. A great deal of care and planning went into the building of this home over a period of four years. The end result includes everything imaginable, including a 22 car underground garage, in a structure that is rustic, masculine in nature, and possesses a great deal of class. The exterior is a well-blended mixture of Adirondack lodges, Gothic cathedrals, English Tudor styling, and a French Chateau.

ARCHITECT: JON R. SAYLER – SPOKANE, WA
BUILDER: DKS CONSTRUCTION SERVICES – WALLA WALLA, WA
INTERIOR DESIGNER: DEBBIE SHAFFER – WALLA WALLA, WA

The Double River
Ranch Residence

*T*he interior construction incorporates a mixture of log post-and-beam with the more traditional framed construction and does a wonderful job of hiding functional necessities such as heating and cooling vents. Australian cypress hardwood tops the floors in the home, while inlaid slate adds color and character to the foyer. Timberline Lodge on Oregon's Mount Hood inspired many of the home's wooden carvings and details. The turret shaped in-home office is accessed from the main structure via a glass-enclosed covered bridge and is heated by a natural wood-burning fireplace.

The open kitchen presents views to the other rooms and promotes a cozy, warm feeling throughout the primary living areas. The massive interior spaces required that everything involving the interior design and decorating had to blend with the space to ensure a comfortable family style of living. Architect Jon Sayler and Interior Designer Debbie Shaffer created a style they refer to as "North Idaho Gothic".

The rear of the home looks out on a spacious swimming pool that enhances the grounds. The views include the luscious valleys of southeastern Washington and the Blue Mountain range in Washington and Oregon.

A poolside cottage includes a sauna, BBQ, recreational area, and also serves as a guest house.

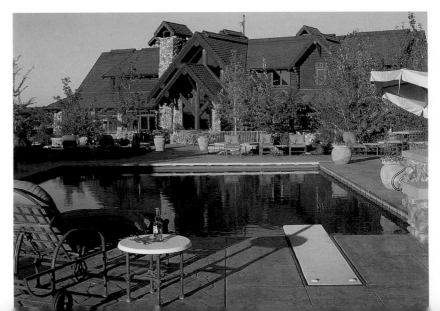

The House at
Eagle Bluff

Photography by Michael Mathers

This gorgeous, contemporary home has style that can best be described as "timeless elegance". Nestled in the wooded foothills of Spokane, Washington, this home appears to be an eruption from the earth that simply belongs there among the natural beauty.

The setting presents a feeling of private serenity and the wonders of Mother Nature. All of the stonework utilizes stone and rock natural to the inland Northwest.

The mountainous terrain and rivers in the surrounding area offers some of the best rafting and hiking opportunities in the Pacific Northwest.

ARCHITECT: JON R. SAYLER – SPOKANE, WA
BUILDER: DANIEL J. OLSON CONSTRUCTION – SPOKANE, WA
INTERIOR DESIGNER: MARA NEWLUN, R. ALAN BROWN – SPOKANE, WA

The interior possesses incredible lighting that is very subtle and provides an atmosphere that is extremely warm and comfortable. A wonderful combination of decorating styles and colors, unique open fireplace, and extensive use of granite and straight grain ash throughout the home, blend nicely to create space that is distinctly family oriented, yet elegant in nature.

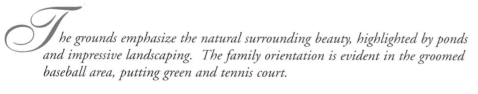
The grounds emphasize the natural surrounding beauty, highlighted by ponds and impressive landscaping. The family orientation is evident in the groomed baseball area, putting green and tennis court.

The owner took great care to make the guest areas in the home special and inviting, as shown here with the custom glass sink and breathtaking view of the surrounding wilderness in the guest bath.

The
DeAtley
Residence

Photography by Steve Young

This fabulous home gives new meaning to the term "custom built". Every detail was meticulously planned out under the careful guidance of renowned architect Vassos M. Demetriou. This masterpiece took four years from start to finish and involved numerous trips to England, Italy and China to select the perfect materials.

Al and Pat DeAtley have always enjoyed the grand homes of Europe with their high ceilings, tall windows and old world charm. With that influence being the predominant theme, they envisioned a home that could be used not only by the family, but also by the community for philanthropic causes. Carved over the main entrance there is a subtle inscription in Latin: *Non Nabis Solum,* meaning *Not Only for Us.*

ARCHITECT & INTERIOR ARCHITECT:
    DEMETRIOU ARCHITECTS – KIRKLAND, WA
BUILDER: KEN MILLER – REDMOND, WA
INTERIOR DESIGNER:
    SHOPKEEFER – YAKIMA, WA

G T O N

49

This is a home with elegant spaces, superb old world design, detail and craftsmanship. The family space for entertaining, both indoors and out, are inviting and spacious, invoking the tradition of old Europe.

This 27,000 square foot home overlooks the Yakima Valley with the Cascade Mountains as a backdrop. The grounds are exquisite, complete with stately fountains, cascading waterfalls, infinity edged pools and a greenhouse from England. Excellent uses of mahogany and cherry wood, along with burl panels, that create rooms which emit elegance, comfort and charm. The state of the art film screening room is modeled after an early 1920's movie theater, complete with stage for live productions, pool table, bar, and hidden drop-down overhead projector.

No wood was used on the exterior of the building, from the slate roof, and stucco and carved stone walls, down to the extensive use of perfectly level pavers designed to keep the exterior areas dry in summer and winter.

The unique wood burning pizza oven was so massive it had to be installed using a crane.

Snyder's Snug Harbor

S T E V E N S O N ,   W A S H I N G T O N

Photography by Michael Mathers

This home was created with a great deal of loving care and attention. Much of the wood throughout the home has over a 100 year history, beginning its evolution as the timbers used in the building of the mighty Bonneville Dam. Thousands of hours went into the recovery, reclamation and refinishing that gives the wood its distinctive distressed appearance.

Located in the magnificent Columbia River Gorge, 60 miles east of Vancouver, Washington, this home provides both unsurpassed scenic beauty and the serenity of a woodland retreat. The blooming of the foliage and flowers in the spring is a site to behold. The unique design, wonderful art, and gorgeous river views makes this home a rewarding treat in all respects.

ARCHITECT & BUILDER: NEIL KELLY DESIGNERS /REMODELERS.- PORTLAND, OR
INTERIOR DESIGN: JANE SNYDER – STEVENSON, WA

Mr. and Mrs. Snyder helped make Snug Harbor what it is today. When the Washington State road crew was faced with the dilemma of what to do with the huge rocks that were being unearthed, the Snyders arranged to absorb the cost of transporting and lining the harbor with these massive boulders.

The fireplace was a custom design constructed using Colorado lead stone with a liberal sprinkling of petrified wood from the Snug Harbor area. A deer hoof print can be seen in the petrified wood that is to the left of the firebox. Glass countertops are an engineering marvel that required untold hours of research and careful fabrication. Back lighting uses fiber optics and a very intricate chipped edge treatment to further diffuse the light emitted from the sculpted glass edges.

The home takes advantage of a geothermal heating system that extracts heat for this large home from the earth and is four times more efficient than conventional electric heating. An elaborate heat recovery system hidden in the walls uses outgoing air to heat incoming air and provides a heat recovery efficiency approaching 90 percent.

The dock extends out over the river to help capture the ever changing and magnificent views presented by the Columbia River Gorge.

55

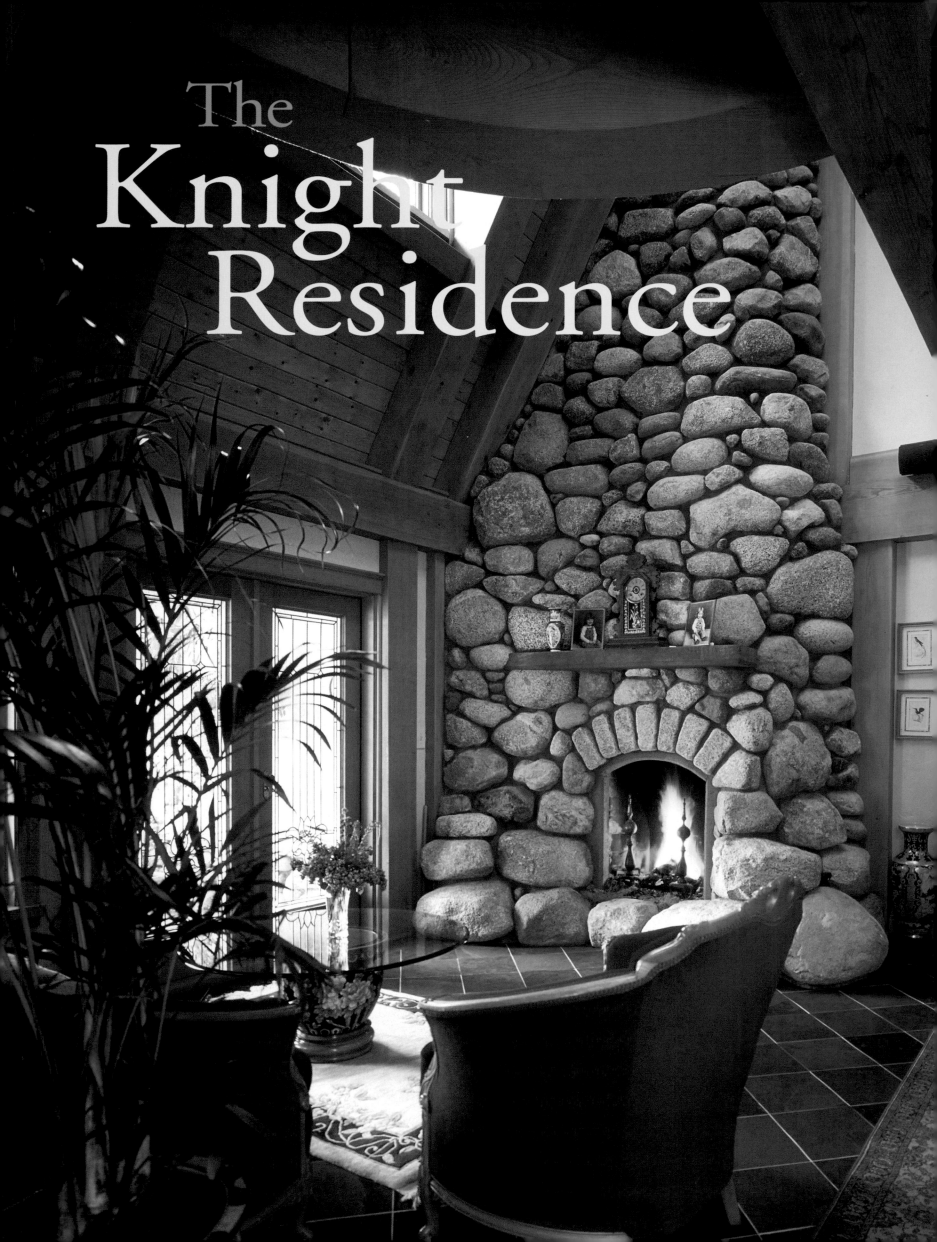

The
Knight
Residence

Photography by Michael Mathers

David and Robin Knight have turned their hobby into a 27 year career they both love, building unique homes one house at a time. Each home has elements of previous ones, yet always incorporate new and different features. Their goal is to create homes that look like they came from another era, when talented artisans could spend the time necessary to make one-of-a-kind homes. Their homes begin with stone foundations that make the home appear to have sprouted from stone and to have been there forever. The rocks of the building flow into the gardens. The surrounding landscape is integrated with the house and defined by retaining walls, pools, and planting borders built of the same rock. The traditional home style includes steep, complicated rooflines. The overall effect is one of solidarity, strength, and security.

ARCHITECT, BUILDER & INTERIOR DESIGN:
DAVID AND ROBIN KNIGHT – FRIDAY HARBOR, WA

Major living areas are designed to focus around their own separate ceiling area, leading to many interesting and different roof angles and pitches.

Dormers and towers make the upstairs bedrooms charming and individually unique. Interior spaces influence the exterior look and are designed to also provide protected entryways and covered deck areas for the home.

*I*nstead of doorways, public rooms have generous openings where the contents of one spill into the next. With the main living spaces overlapping one another, the result is longer views and a sense of inclusion. Heavy timbers and stone give the areas substantial bearing that is also snug and cozy. The home also delights with decorative features involving leaded glass, shaped rafted ends and intricate stucco patterns. Every window in the home is made using stained and leaded glass windows.

Spread information source:
Fine Home Building, Summer 2002

The Fanch Retreat
at Wing Point

BAINBRIDGE, WASHINGTON

Photography by Michael Mathers

Located at the very tip of Wing Point on Bainbridge Island, this home is the epitome of the home selection criteria, "location - location - location". With 330 degrees of captivating, world-class views, this location is second to none.

From the golden aura of sunrise over the cityscape of Seattle, to the twinkling of city night-lights and star-studded skies, the views are nothing less than breathtaking. A cozy bench on the point at the very tip of the land presents everything the Sound has to offer, as well as unparalleled views of both Mt. Baker and Mt. Rainier.

ARCHITECT & BUILDER: 1901 – THE BLACK FAMILY

*E*veryone traveling to Bainbridge Island by ferry gets a bird's eye view of the property on the right side, as they are about to enter the port. The distinguished flagpole placed by Senator Magnuson at the extreme tip is usually the first sight many visitors to the island will see.

Remodeled by the Senator, the home now belongs to the Fanch family who furnished it to suit their warm and comfortable family oriented lifestyle.

The home is almost hidden from view by the towering trees and lush landscaping, providing a feeling of privacy and serenity with a window to the world.

Cozy on
Bainbridge
Island

B A I N B R I D G E   I S L A N D,   W A

Photography by Michael Mathers

This quaint beachfront cottage on the Sound has it all; style, comfort and majestic views. The owners worked closely with the architect and builder to create a cozy family retreat that is truly unique and comfortable. The architect, Peter Brachvogel AIA, refers to his creation as "a whimsical interpretation of a 1920's cottage by the sea". The home is complemented magnificently by the impressive landscaping with the perfect combination of plants and foliage to accentuate the home and its wonderful setting. One of the Northwest's premier landscape artists, Patrick Leuner, took great care to compliment the exterior grounds with the perfect combination of plants and foliage to accentuate the home and its wonderful setting.

ARCHITECT: BC&J ARCHITECTURE/PETER BRACHVOGEL, AIA, PRINCIPAL IN CHARGE – BAINBRIDGE ISLAND, WA
BUILDER: W.M. CORBIN CONSTRUCTION CORP. – BAINBRIDGE ISLAND, WA

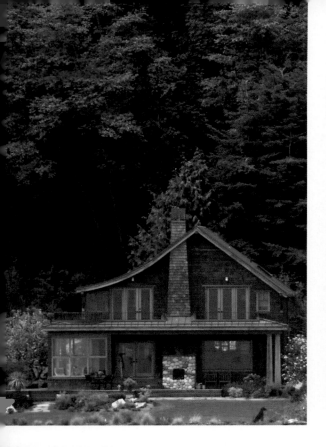

A glass walled dining area that juts off by the kitchen and family room provides for casual dining while enjoying all that Puget Sound and the Seattle skyline have to offer.

Directly above the glass enclosed dining area is an open air, rounded balcony off the master bedroom. The balcony rewards individuals with an impressive view of the Sound, Mt. Baker, and Mt. Rainier. Lots of beachfront decking makes for further enjoyment of these intoxicating views.

The craftsmanship that has gone into the wood-working is nothing short of fabulous, right down to the lighthouse shaped stairway and banister posts. This nautical theme is used in many areas, utilizing a ship's ladder to reach a loft sleeping area, and to provide a Cape Cod type environ-ment throughout the home. The guesthouse and garage continue the New England beach house ambiance.

The End of the
Rainbow

First trial runs, October 1949 on Lake Washington, reached 150-160 miles per hour.

The property was a marvel of its time, designed by internationally renowned architect, Roland Terry, the "father of Northwest architecture", who created unique, grand spaces with understated luxury.

HUNTS POINT, WASHINGTON

Photography by Michael Mathers

This stunning Hunt's Point waterfront property is the jewel of Lake Washington. This two acre level parcel of land encompasses the entire tip of Hunt's Point, has 846 linear feet of prime Lake Washington waterfront, and offers 270 degree views that include the Seattle skyline and surrounding mountains. This 6,860 square foot home was built in 1950 by the pioneer of Seattle hydroplane racing, Stan Sayers.

Stan Sayers is regarded as the individual responsible for bringing hydroplane racing superiority to Seattle. The city fathers invented *SEAFAIR* as a summer celebration focal point for the community, but lacked a headline event to draw the crowds until Sayers took his locally designed, record setting Slo-mo-shun IV hydroplane to Detroit and brought home the prestigious Gold Cup trophy to Seattle. Slo-mo-shun IV held onto the cup for five straight years, providing Seattle with the impetus to launch and establish the SeaFair as one of the nation's most outstanding summer events. The Slo-mo-shun IV racing team became a rallying point for the city, and with the boat being moored at Hunts Point, this property quickly became the place for post race celebrations and the center of the Seattle racing world.

ARCHITECT: ROLAND TERRY – SEATTLE, WA

B/W Photos: Opposite page and below by Mary Randlett

Stan Sayers and Anchor Jensen preparing for Slo-mo-shun IV first test run. (1949)

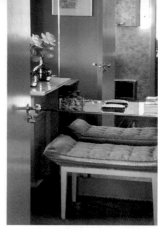

The glass walled sunken living room was built with enough room for two grand pianos and provides light filled openness. The property includes many amenities; impressive marble fireplace, spacious manicured lawns, expansive gardens, very private pool area, historical boathouse and dock, and a swimming cove with a sandy beach. These are but a few examples that demonstrate why this exquisite home is regarded as one of the most notable sites in North America and has earned it the title of "The End of the Rainbow".

The home boasts great attention to style and detail with custom features like this fish-shaped swimming pool.

WESTERN NORTHERN SOUTHERN WESTERN NORTHERN SOUTHERN WESTERN NORTHERN SOUTHERN WESTERN

A collection of Oregon's most original and distinctive homes.

NORTHERN

Spanish Style on Fremont Street, The Manion Home, The Aqua Star, High Above the Willamette, Serene Retreat, Twin Points Peninsula, Elk Rock Road Residence, Batke-Niemi Residence

SOUTHERN

At Home on the Ranch, The Villa at John's Peak

WESTERN

Mollie B - By the Sea, Pigeon Point Beach House

The magnificent State of Oregon is like four worlds in one. From the stormy Pacific Ocean coastline to the high desert areas of Eastern Oregon, a person is presented with a wide array of scenic beauty. The lush Oregon valleys and majestic mountains in-between provide views that tend to leave one simply awestruck.

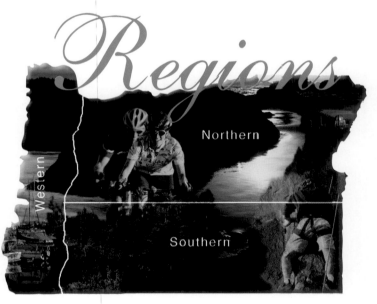

Within this wonderland provided by Mother Nature, a person can also find some amazing man-made structures. The following pages reward the reader with displays of homes that can only be imagined in your wildest dreams. Homes that are perched atop a ship's mast, a coastal beach house, lakefront masterpieces, as well as worldly mansions and villas are but some of the inspiring homes presented for your enjoyment in this section.

Spanish Style on
Fremont
Street

PORTLAND, OREGON

Photography by Michael Mathers

This 1926 Spanish beauty was virtually built around a collection of striking, European stained-glass leaded windows. Designs depict everything from damsels in distress and handsome knights to brilliant floral displays. The interior style is minimalist throughout the home, reducing detail to the most treasured items, such as the Chinese earthenware vessel, a set of free standing Sante Fe pillars, matching leather sofas, and faux zebra rug shown in this intriguingly beautiful great room.

ARCHITECT: HAROLD TAYLOR - PORTLAND, OR
BUILDER: JOHN ADAMS - PORTLAND, OR

The bedroom features a faux zebra bedspread, a Joan Miro rug, and wire chairs of a 1952 award winning design that won a place in the Museum of Modern Fine Art.

The owners' favorite objet d'art is his replication of a cover shot used by the Architectural Digest magazine. He was proud to say that his rendition is "not like the wall, it is the wall". The entire home is filled with art and stands alone as a work of art in its own right.

The exterior of this home is living art at its best. The home is nestled in one of Portland's most beloved gardens. The thousands who enjoy it on a regular basis feel it is well worth the 50 or more hours a week it requires to maintain its beauty. The classic pink stucco, Spanish style home and setting would grace its surroundings whether it were located in Portland, Beverly Hills, or Madrid, Spain.

The hot tub area gives one the feeling of being in a tropical paradise, with exotic plants, foliage and plenty of natural light.

77

The Manion Home

Photography by Michael Mathers

High atop the cliffs overlooking the ever-amazing Columbia River Gorge, this stunning contemporary home is a sight to behold. Built in 1998, it was designed to look like something out of the 18th century. The home was inspired by the *estancia* in the splendid rural estates of Argentina, with subtle nuances of Spain, England, France, Italy, Scotland, and the Pacific Northwest to add emphasis in all the right places.

Dubbed "Villa Mandala" by its owners, this centuries old looking home, with its virtually colorless "Roman cement" exterior, sits on 40 acres of land that possesses some of the most exquisite views in the world and is surrounded by creeks, pure water falls and forever green Oregon foliage. The oversized French entry doors are but one example of the owner's superior wood crafting skills. His upscale cabinetry, furniture and designer pieces are found in many homes in the region.

ARCHITECT, BUILDER & INTERIOR DESIGNER:
SANDY & MIKE MANION – CORBETT, OR

The interior is a tribute to the owners' decorating skills and is best described as "informal elegance". The home is flooded with colors, including watermelon, curry, pistachio, hazelnut, lime and persimmon butter, all of which help to emphasize the Northwest art and interior details.

The flooring ranges from tumbled limestone, to lend a European formality, to beautifully burnished salvaged cherry. Color warms up every room, brightens the sensations and is ever present to impart the estancia style.

Spread information source: Northwest Style

The Aqua Star
Living on the Willamette

Photography by Adam Bacher

Frank Lloyd Wright was a great believer in his creations, "Living within the spirit and environment of their settings".

The "Aqua Star" emerges from the water with corners resembling waves and metal with transparent reflective qualities similar to water. Removed from the river, it would not come alive; it requires the light and movement the river provides. The "Aqua Star" shows its appreciation by serving as a mirror to the river's many moods. The summer sunsets paint it pink, while the rain showers turn it into a shiny jewel.

The home welcomes people and entertains in both the grand sense and the intimate. Unconventional materials provide a clear canvas in which to translate eclectic to elegant taste and allow one to easily transform the atmosphere to suit the moment.

ARCHITECT: LARRY HART – PORTLAND, OREGON
BUILDER: BUZZ GORDER – PORTLAND, OREGON
DESIGNER: BUZZ GORDER – PORTLAND, OREGON

Inside, the paraline walls intensify light and mirror colors from surrounding flowers and the ever-changing waters. Suspended art dances in reaction to river traffic, while high ceilings accommodate large paintings or a 15 foot Christmas tree.

*S*urrounding windows provide a 360-degree view that encompass a bridge, an island complete with eagles, the Portland skyline, and playful otters cavorting nearby. The seasons offer Christmas flotillas, salmon fishing, and the intense pulse of summer. Easy access to water and an abundance of water toys provide an exciting change of pace available to all in a matter of seconds. "A constant vacation" has often been evoked to describe this unique and wonderful lifestyle.

High Above the
Willamette

PORTLAND, OREGON

Photography by Michael Mathers

This spectacular round living space, 26 floors above downtown Portland, is actually two condos combined into a 2,700 square foot unit with an absolutely stunning 260-degree view. The panoramic view includes the Willamette River, Mt. Hood, the greenery of the surrounding area, and a nighttime skyline that mimics New York City. The beautiful views can be seen from every room.

The residence's construction was designed to match the style of the stainless, three-pod exterior of the high-rise. The inside round walls provide symmetry with the exterior. The black granite floors mirror the shine of the reflecting windows. The kitchen maintains a black-and-white look that remains modern, but allows the owner to customize colors depending on the season.

This home plays up its downtown roots and speaks of nothing but contemporary. The unit has been extensively remodeled to include state-of-the-art entertainment systems, custom-built mahogany cabinets, and light from different sources that give the condo the feel of an outside space.

The main dining area also serves as a conference space with seating for eight around the high-gloss, custom Mirak table. The transparent lit cabinets let crystal wine glasses sparkle, and black granite under lit counters compliment the stainless bar sink, complete with beer tap and crystal decanters.

The master bedroom has been elevated a few steps to allow viewing of the river from the bed. The dropped ceiling around the windows allows the room to feel cozy, customized and comfortable; the direct lighting over the artwork adds to the effect. The master bath area includes an oversized jacuzzi tub with waterfall and jets, a steam-room in the large shower, and sauna for two.

Add to all of this the swimming pool, exercise room, party facilities, and other building amenities and "High Above the Willamette" is a very comfortable and beautiful place to be.

Serene Retreat

Opposite:
This octagonal shaped architectural miracle is three-quarter glass. In addition to windows all around, four large sky-lights are positioned between the metal ceiling struts to provide even more light.

Photography by Michael Mathers

uilt atop a 60-foot mast from the WWII navy ship USS James O'Hara, this architectural marvel offers extraordinary views of the Portland cityscape and three majestic mountains. The sun rising over Mt. Hood presents an absolutely spectacular view each morning. Steel beam horizontal stabilizers are driven into the hillside at the main floor level, and a 40-foot square concrete pad supported by nine steel pilings secured in rock, supports the mast itself. Structural engineers claim the house is "braced into the next century and beyond".

Few homes are more unique than this creative structure, which grabs the attention of virtually everyone, including Hollywood film makers who used this home as the setting for the film *Hear No Evil*, starring Martin Sheen and Marlee Matlin.

ARCHITECT: ZAIK/MILLER ASSOCIATES ARCHITECTS/PLANNERS – PORTLAND, OR
BUILDER : BARNARD & KINNEY – PORTLAND, OR

The stabilizing beams support a garage and a gated entryway, and provide level access to the slated entry. This area also includes an amazingly beautiful Kurisu Japanese garden, complete with ponds and two waterfalls. The garden, which continues on down the sloping hillside, took four years to complete.

Natural materials are an interior focus, with custom-made tables of marble, glass and granite. A spiral staircase winds around the mast to the lower level sitting room, guest bedroom and bath.

Twin Points Peninsula

A distinctively unique 1,400 square foot studio was recently added to the remodeled boathouse and lends itself to the perfect creative environment. The play of light off the water through the wall of glass is spectacular. Quite often herons and eagles are spotted soaring above the private bay, adding to the peaceful serenity of the setting.

Photography by Michael Mathers

This spectacular home sits on a 2.3 acre peninsula in the prestigious Lake Oswego area, with lake views in three directions. The house is a contemporary blend of Asian and Frank Lloyd Wright influences. A hand-made blue tile Japanese roof, complete with magnificent ceramic fish sculptures, crowns this one-of-a-kind home. A Kurisu designed Japanese garden, complete with a koi pond and a waterfall with a bridge, is among several gardens connected by stone and gravel pathways.

ARCHITECTS: NEIL KELLY / DESIGNERS & REMODELERS – PORTLAND, OR
BUILDER: NEIL KELLY / DESIGNERS & REMODELERS – PORTLAND, OR

Left: Stone stairs lead down to the waterfront and two docks. Patios, a large deck, and wonderful lakeside lawn and garden areas accommodate up to 200 people.

A green slate entryway leads one inside to the beauty of open spaces separated by sliding room screens made of fir and stained glass. An attractive use of color blends well with impressive mahogany floors with maple inlays.

A massive Feather River Rock fireplace is the focal point of the main living room area. Cabinetry made of Bubinga, African hardwood, and bird's-eye maple is seen throughout the kitchen and dining areas.

The Pigeon Point Beach House

House

GOLD BEACH, OREGON

Photography by Tom Rider

The driftwood logs that have been deposited on the beach over the years by blustery Oregon coastal storms inspired this unique beach house. This massive, triangular shaped home is located on the rugged Gold Beach, Oregon coast and was built to withstand winds of up to 100 miles per hour. The local Port Orford cedar logs used on the interior and exterior construction were selected for their strength, resistance to water damage, and natural beauty.

This architectural creation sizzles with originality. The site-specific design promotes a reflection of the nature of the landscape it occupies. The style pushes the envelope of traditional construction techniques and uses unconventional materials to manifest individuality in this one-of-a-kind residence.

ARCHITECT: OBIE BOWMAN, AIA –
HEALDSBURG, CA
BUILDER: JOHN HARPER, NOMAD DESIGN –
GOLD BEACH, OR

Above: Triangular floor plan points the prow-like nose of the structure out to sea, with glass walls facing northwest and southwest to allow a 180-degree view of the coastline.

The house progresses from a secure sense of shelter in the bedroom and kitchen areas, to one of almost complete exposure, with the ceiling and windows rising as they propel themselves toward the view. The very tip of the expansive living room culminates with a glass walled loft, which serves as an ideal spot for observing the massive waves of a winter storm, while also serving as a protective shelter for the ocean-side entry below.

Top: A pair of barn-doors by the entry way can be pulled together and secured while away or to block stormy weather.

At Home
on the Ranch

BEND, OREGON

Photography by Michael Mathers

The Vandervert Ranch has a rich history dating back to 1892, when W. P. Vandervert returned to Oregon to buy 400 acres and build the "Old Homestead". Including the guesthouse, another log and stone structure, this 4,251 square foot historic legacy has been nationally recognized in Architectural Digest (June 1998). The residence is one of exceptional quality in an environment of great natural beauty.

An Adirondack-style log gated entrance welcomes you to miles of crystal clear, trout filled, Little Deschutes River, lush open meadows, stately forest, and magnificent snowcapped mountain vistas. The "Old Homestead" has views of Mt. Bachelor, Broken Top, Paulina Peak and Three Sisters Mountains.

ARCHITECT: NEAL HUSTON ARCHITECT – BEND, OR
BUILDER/RESTORATION: ED ADAMS/HANDCRAFTED LOG HOMES
   SISTERS, OR
INTERIOR DESIGNER: GARDNER ASSOCIATES

The Rustic Camas Basalt fireplace, massive log and beam interior, and high ceiling give the home a grand and majestic feeling. "Rustic Elegance" is the theme, right down to the saddles on the loft balcony railing to the antique furnishings and country views.

The master bedroom centerpiece is an 1890 Victorian bed. It is surrounded by the warm feel of natural wood and is enhanced by modern conveniences. Unique custom ironwork by the late Russ Maugins (famous for his work on the historic Timberline Lodge) is also a highlight of the "Old Homestead".

Bottom right: Zelda greets guests to the "Old Homestead" and guards the owner's collection of vintage cowboy boots and hats in the entryway.

The Villa at
John's Peak

Left: Expansive 14-foot ceiling, cove lighting and the French-style antique chandelier unify this luxurious living space. The genuine plaster walls were created with color mixed in to present a warm and natural atmosphere.

JACKSONVILLE, OREGON

Photo above by Kim Budd

Photography by Mark Mularz

This warm and welcoming home provides an open and sunny living space with an inviting floor plan spanning over 7,540 square feet. The sophisticated European architecture is reminiscent of an exquisite French Mediterranean Villa, situated on 20 acres that crest the West Hills of Southern Oregon. The views are absolutely stunning, and the natural surroundings provide a magnificent sense of freedom. Nestled comfortably in a secured gated community, it's still just minutes away from the conveniences of town.

DESIGN ARCHITECT: MICHAEL HELM ARCHITECTS LTD –
   TORTOLA, BRITISH VIRGIN ISLANDS
ARCHITECT: BRUCE W. RICHEY, AIA – MEDFORD, OREGON
BUILDER: HARTSOOK CONSTRUCTION – MEDFORD, OREGON

This estate offers one of the finest gourmet kitchens imaginable, featuring solid granite countertops and three separate islands. Fully equipped, the state-of-the-art appliances include two convection ovens and a six-burner cooktop griddle.

Top left: The pantry area is enclosed with stained-glass doors; custom cabinetry and domed skylight complete the space.

There is also an adjacent wine-tasting room, with everything designed to be visually integrated into the great room.

All living areas in the home have patios adjacent, offering spectacular views. The upper-level patio lovingly displays four hand-carved pillars from Nepal. The home features authentic stucco exterior, while the antique brickwork used in the interior simulates the arches found in historic downtown Jacksonville.

*T*he clay tile roof complements the overall design and feel of this authentic setting. The swimming pool has an infinity edge and waterfall, with Italian porcelain-tiled deck and mahogany bridge to further enhance the surrounding views. The well-appointed landscaping features, including the climate-controlled greenhouse, put the finishing touches on this idyllic setting and make for perfect outdoor living and entertaining.

SALISHAN, OREGON

Photography by Michael Mathers

This wonderful vacation home on the beach was inspired by the 50's hit, "See the Pyramids Along the Nile". The end result is a unique home with three central pyramid pods, each with a distinctive zone for activities. The home is built on a special site that is a sand spit separating the Pacific Ocean and Siletz Bay, where sea lions bask on the beach and cavort in the water. Whales can be seen migrating not far off shore. This special place maintains a harmonious relationship with the sand and the sea, and provides everyone with a graceful feeling of serenity.

Mollie B
By the Sea

ARCHITECT: R.G. NELSON – COEUR D'ALENE, ID
BUILDER: BARDEN CONSTRUCTION – LINCOLN CITY, OR
INTERIOR DESIGNERS:
   R.G. NELSON – COEUR D'ALENE, ID
   LESLIE DRESSEL – LINCOLN CITY, OR

The community area is the focal point of the home and possesses a very comfortable, family oriented style. The children's bedroom loft fits well with the general family elegance theme. The front door is a custom sculpture of wood and ceramic, mirroring the rich, dewy colors and watery images of Salishan.

$\mathcal{E}$ very room in the home has access to water views and the ethereal vistas offered by the Bay and the Ocean. A rectangular marble table on wheels extends out from the kitchen wall to seat up to 12, and then recesses out of the way when not in use. Interior and exterior cedar woods are finished with craftsman precision.

Top right: Television sets rise out of an Italian designed floor chest, and chic, understated furnishings dress the home in style and class.

LAKE OSWEGO, OREGON

Photography by Michael Mathers

Appearing to soar right out of the hillside, this house clings to a 30-degree slope rising above the Willamette River, providing a spectacular view of the river, Mt. Hood, and the rising sun. The house has been described as an "experiment in feelings". Although providing a secure feeling of being anchored into the site, the structure achieves a sensation of floating in space, much like a bird in flight. The home is funnel-like in shape: starting out with a small studio on the lowest level, moving to the children's bedrooms on the middle level, and on the upper level, where the view is the best, family community spaces and the master bedroom suite.

ARCHITECT, BUILDER & INTERIOR DESIGNER:
ROBERT H. OSHATZ – PORTLAND, OR

Elk
Rock Road
Residence

*R*obert Harvey Oshatz's architectural designs exemplify the term "unique". Known for his unconventional and intriguing designs, his work has been described as "organic, green architecture, sustainable, exotic, futuristic, and extreme". His goal is to capture the owners' emotion and have them be moved emotionally by the ambiance of their home. With every structure, he creates a piece of art, wherein the poetry of the site is reflected in the poetry of the architecture.

*T*he interior spaces of this 3,500 square foot home feature slate and carpet floors, white oak cabinets with granite counters, hemlock ceilings, custom beveled cedar walls, and built-in window seats along the outer walls to partake of the panoramic view.

The exterior is woven together with custom beveled cedar siding, brown stone from central Oregon and teal colored stucco.

The
Batke & Niemi
Residence

P O R T L A N D ,   O R E G O N

Photography by Michael Mathers,
Holly Stickley, and Strode Eckert Photography

The sophisticated contemporary style of this home is the wonderful creation of its owners and demonstrates the beauty that results when an artistic interior designer and a creative architect join forces.

Eclectic art and classical architecture combine to create this exquisite masterpiece. Mediterranean elements begin at the front entry. The entry is tiled and walled in the style of a European courtyard.

ARCHITECT & BUILDER:
  DENNIS BATKE ARCHITECTURE – PORTLAND, OR
INTERIOR DESINGER:
  KAROL NIEMI – PORTLAND, OR

*T*he floors are inlaid with exotic woods, carpeted in geometric designs, or laid using elegant rectangles of black-and-white tile.

This Northwest Portland home boasts views of four mountains, with the magnificent Mt. Hood framed perfectly by the dining room's double-glass doors.

*T*his four level home reminds one of a villa in Portofino with its elegant materials, contemporary art, and rare antiques collected from around the world.

Stair risers are set in bands of black-and-white recycled marble tile the size of piano keys. The Italian coffee table with extensive European glass collection, oil painting above the mantel, and glass-art objects are the perfect accents to this stunning black-and-white emphasis.

The home's bold color scheme is energized with shots of saturated color: nasturtium, gold, orange juice, warm pewter, and firecracker red.

Spread information source: Northwest Style

UNIQUE HOMES OF
Idaho

A collection of Idaho's most original and distinctive homes.

*I*daho is one of the world's best-kept secrets. Beyond its rural "famous potatoes" image, Idaho is comprised of towering peaks, some of the best skiing in the world, world class white water rafting, unheralded fresh water fishing, pristine lakes, and endless hiking trails, the sum of which equals a quality of life standard that is unsurpassed anywhere.

Nestled among Idaho's spectacular locations are private homes that most would not believe even existed. The elite few who have discovered this state's immeasurable virtues have constructed the likes of a 30,000 square foot home, a ski chateau, a lakefront home built on a rock, and even a remarkable tree house fit for royalty, just to name a few. Some of Idaho's beautiful homes and artistic creations have been provided in the following pages for your viewing pleasure.

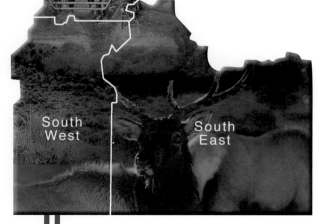

NORTHERN

Hagadone House, Moore House, Healy Tree House, The Cloninger House

SOUTHWEST

House at Eagle's Perch, Hetland House, Robie Springs House, Comstock Townhouse

SOUTHEAST

Chelonia, Drackett House, House at Eagle Creek, Ellis House

The Hagadone House

COEUR D'ALENE, IDAHO

Photography by Quicksilver Studios

Overlooking Lake Coeur d'Alene in North Idaho, this internationally styled Hagadone home was designed to incorporate materials from around the globe. There is a great use of exotic woods including: Mahogany Chenille, Bubinga Wood and quartered African Satinwood, Sycamore and Santos. The woods are combined in harmonious patterns and are accented by the stonework created with materials imported from Italy, France, Germany, South America and Asia. The home occupies a 16-acre site on Stanley Hill above the city of Coeur d'Alene, and the complex consists of approximately 30,000 square feet. It also includes an adjacent indoor

ARCHITECT: WARREN SHEETS • BUILDER: PANCO CONSTRUCTION

125

tennis court (which can be converted to a banquet facility for up to 550 guests), a driving range with putting green, an 11-car garage and caretaker facilities. The home features 10 fireplaces, 17 bathrooms, indoor and outdoor tennis courts and swimming pools, a complete recreation center with a fully-automated bowling alley, and extensive waterscape features such as serenity pools, waterfalls and fountains.

Multiple views of the Hagadone House: (Opposite, clockwise from top) Aerial views; exterior at dusk; living room; dining room; pool at night. (Clockwise from top left) Bar, library, kitchen, bathroom. Warren Sheets Design of San Francisco fashioned the interior, which transforms raw space into sensual art.

The Moore House

COEUR D'ALENE, IDAHO

Photography by Quicksilver Studios

The Moore House on Lake Coeur d'Alene sits at the very tip of Arrow Point on a basalt rock outcropping. Built in 1970 as a summer cottage, the house has been remodeled to emphasize the view and enhance its spaciousness. The 2,000 square foot house is finished with a pale grey interior to show off the natural blues and greens of the lake that surrounds on three sides. The furnishings are low profile and accented by a collection of nude sculptures in black and white.

ARCHITECT: ELMER JORDAN -
COEUR D' ALENE, ID
BUILDER: ALLAN EBORALL -
COEUR D' ALENE, ID

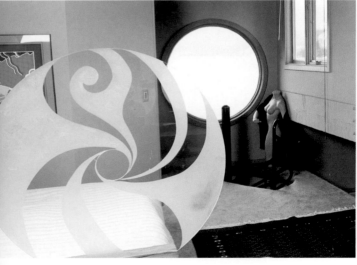

Above left: A round port-hole-like window was added in the loft. Above right: The remodeled bathroom features a steam bath with a lake view.

Clean, contemporary lines are evident throughout all levels of the house on the lake, both in the interior structural design and the stylish furnishings shown on these pages.

The Healy
Tree House

SANDPOINT, IDAHO

The Healy Tree House is "livable art" perched high in the branches of three massive trees on Lake Pend Oreille near Sandpoint. The tree house was conceived of, and built by Jim and Deanne Healy to inspire childlike awe at the wonders of nature. From the entrance stairway that swings into the tree limbs on a sandbag counterbalance, to the lookout tower forty-seven feet above the ground, this nest of a house invites its guests to revel in whimsy.

ARCHITECT & BUILDER:
 JIM & DEANNE HEALY - SANDPOINT, ID

Photography by Quicksilver Studios

Inspired by the architect Gaudi of Spain, the soft curves of the only new windows in the house merge the room subtly with the panorama.

An African fertility pole and hand-hewn plank staircase extended by boat ladders provide an invitation to the upper levels.

The king bed in the second-level nook provides luxurious lake views, while the third level entertains those younger at heart with stargazing and wildlife viewings.

The living room, kitchen and bathroom are located on the first level. Antique leaded windows from England, portholes and memorabilia from Valentino's yacht, a bathroom wrapped with copper walls, and natural slate floors highlight the living spaces.

135

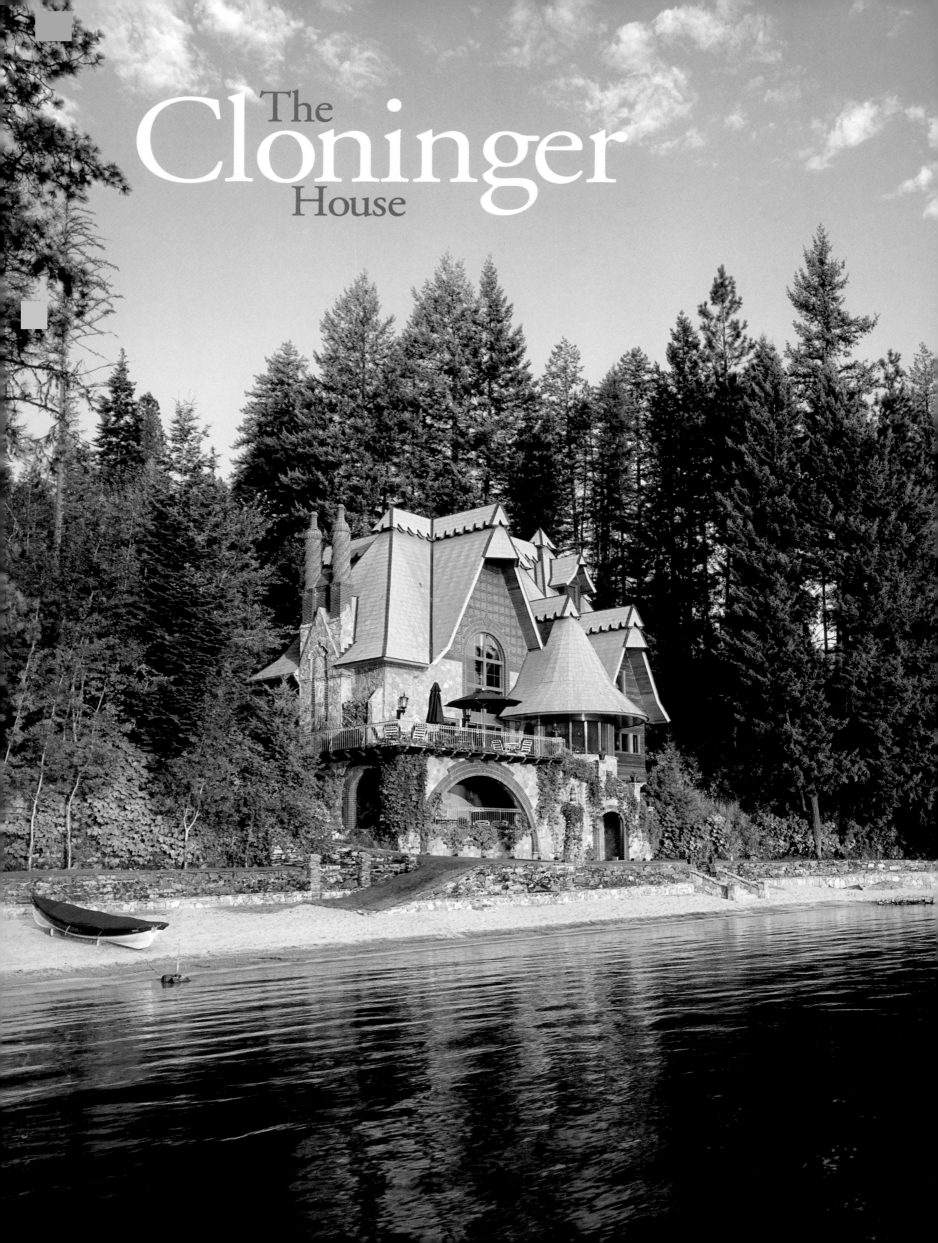

The Cloninger
House
The

The
Cloninger
House

COEUR D'ALENE, IDAHO

Photography by Quicksilver Studios

This unique home brings extra magic to a summer cruise along the shores of Northern Idaho's Lake Coeur d'Alene. The trees at maximum foliage, air vibrant with blossoming flowers, and water shimmering with morning's soft light create the backdrop for Cloninger's stately, charming stone cottage that beckons guests ashore. Dubbed "Toad Hall," from *The Wind in the Willows,* this finely crafted blend of steel, concrete, stone, Northwest pine, fir, alder, and cedar seems to whisper, "Come inside and explore."

ARCHITECT & BUILDER: GLEN CLONINGER - SPOKANE, WA

*G*len and Pam Cloninger wanted a lake cabin possessing historic flavor and this home with its unique design featuring a witch-hat roof top, turrets, stone archways, twisting brick chimneys, coffered ceilings, and window seats, charmingly epitomizes their goal.

* Spread information source: Coeur d'Alene Magazine, Summer 2001

The clever design makes the home appear more spacious than the actual square footage, while projecting a much larger feeling due to the roof's steep expanse. At 60 degrees, this roof is the steepest pitch architect Cloninger has ever designed.

This unique house was a construction challenge, having wood beams embedded in stone and staircases buried in bedrock. Master stone masons George Sherman and Johnny Fry built the walls of Idaho granite.

The House at
Eagle's Perch

BOISE, IDAHO

*E*agle's Perch, constructed of quarried sandstone from the Idaho foothills, is nestled on five acres of the banks of the Boise River. The fifty-foot roof of thatched cedar shake rises above the landscaped estate with raised rock gardens, quarried sandstone rose gardens and fifty-foot cottonwood, Russian olive and copper rose trees.

The home features nine-foot pewter doors, limestone flooring, eighteen-foot arched windows and a magnificent free-hanging spiral staircase. With 13,000 square feet of living space, this elegant home offers a Great Room featuring the *Eagle's Perch on the River* sculpture, an oak-paneled library, a formal dining room with silk wall coverings, a 500-bottle-storage wine cellar, a master bedroom with a Brazilian black granite fireplace and a 30 x 50 foot recreation room overlooking the stream and river below. The grounds boast a vine-covered arbor, high-tech greenhouse and custom-engineered streams and ponds that attract nesting bald eagles.

The kitchen is a gourmet's dream with a six-by-ten foot granite island and a custom oak china hutch with beveled glass doors accented by the polished slat oak flooring. A charming view of the stone and herringbone tile bi-level patio is offered through the nine-foot bay window in the breakfast nook.

A magnificent fourteen-foot stone and granite fireplace with a custom oak mantel warms the family room with its coffered oak ceilings and fabric and oak wall coverings.

Photography by Phil McClain

ARCHITECT: BRS ARCHITECTS - BOISE, ID
BUILDER: RANDY HEMMER - BOISE, ID

Like the eagles that perch nearby, the English Tudor house sits grandly on the Boise River. Architect Tim Terry's design concept captured the site's main feature "the Boise River" by incorporating a lineal designed floor plan. By reflecting the lineal nature of the river, the house invites views to the river from every room.

"It took a team effort with the architect, owners, interior designer and my crews to create this one of a kind, timeless estate. It was a wonderful experience," says builder Randy Hemmer of Randy Hemmer Construction L.L.C.

Inside the solid pewter doors of Eagle's Perch are the traditional trappings of elegance—towering ceilings, a spiral staircase, (opposite far left) and brilliant oriental rugs. With the desire to entertain large groups of people, the design utilizes wide corridors linking all the main living areas. The main living room displays enormous glass and concrete artwork by Laddie John Dill.

There is unique intergrated roof venting within the random shake-styled roof and separate, complete groundskeepers quarters over the garage. Locally quarried sandstone is used internally and externally.

The Hetland House

B O I S E ,   I D A H O

Photography by Phil McClain

The Hetland home perches in the Boise foothills overlooking Hulls Gulch offering a panoramic view of the Treasure Valley. This southwestern-styled gem is a three-story structure built by J Bar K and Associates that combines the elements of shape, color and texture to achieve its overall effect. The grand entrance hall features a mosaic tile "rug" accented by rich, warm walls. Recessed shelving built in with curves and flowing lines provides natural frameworks for books and the artwork that adorns the home. The colors of local artist Tony Ball feature sunrises and sunsets that enhance the southwest décor.

ARCHITECT: SCOTT KAMM - BOISE, ID
BUILDER: J BAR K - EAGLE, ID

Bottom: The backyard landscape capitalizes on the southwestern theme with its curving swimming pool accentuated by low-growing shrubbery, a slate walk and stonework.

*T*he exterior of the home is
a study in the clean lines of
southwestern architecture
accentuated by the graceful
curve of the turret and the
subtle rise of the three stories.

The House at
Robie Springs

Architect Dennis Stevens: A Legacy and the Land

J R O B I E S P R I N G S , I D A H O

Just half an hour from downtown Boise, amid the rugged mountains of Idaho's Robie Creek, a master architect is quietly fulfilling a vision . . . 15 homes covering 50 acres.

Dennis Stephens, a direct disciple of legendary architect Frank Lloyd Wright, is designing all the homes to be part of the environment. The community will have no fences and no visible boundaries. It will be an example of modern habitation harmoniously integrated with a natural wilderness landscape.

This remarkable two-level, 5,000 square-foot home grows out of the hill and follows the land's natural slope while offering multiple breathtaking views. Even indoors there is no sense of enclosure, just interaction between nature and home.

The materials, tones, and textures of the inside of the home reflect the natural elements and visual lines outside of it. "Living in a concept," Stevens calls it. "If it looks like it's been here for 50 years, I've done my job."

Though the structure is anchored 12 feet into granite with 650 anchor bolts, the house floats freely, creating a feeling of movement and reinforcing the symbolic interaction with its surroundings.

ARCHITECT: DENNIS STEVENS - ROBIE SPRINGS, ID
BUILDER: ARCHITECTURAL ENTERPRISES, LTD - ROBIE SPRINGS, ID

Photography by Phil McClain

*R*obie Springs is an opportunity to show the world that homes and nature can exist harmoniously when approached with a conscientious design and respect for the land. Before beginning the Robie Springs project, Architect Stevens and his wife, Jackie, undertook a three-year search—considering Colorado, New Mexico, and Arizona before falling in love with Idaho's Robie Creek region.

The various elements and room blend, overlap, integrate, and weave wonderfully throughout both floors in this clean, contemporary design.

At age 17, Robie Springs architect Dennis Stevens was one of legendary architect Frank Lloyd Wright's youngest apprentices. Stevens lived and worked with Wright over a period of five years.

UPTOWN LIVING
The Comstock Townhouse

BOISE, IDAHO

The Comstock Townhouse overlooks the city of Boise from the top floor of the Washington Mutual building. The condominium, at just over 2,300 square feet, is a unique accomplishment in melding the look and feel of old and new world styles to provide a true metropolitan experience. It is finished with a natural palette of materials, and the designer's eye for detail was critical to finessing everything from craftsmanship to colors in this relatively small space with an expansive feel.

The entryway to the two-story loft home gives way to the kitchen, which is styled after a restaurant on a quaint Italian street. This ambience is accented by a charming table for two and marble countertops (crafted from the same marble used in the Washington Monument) and limestone treatments. From the kitchen, the hallway

Photography by Phil McClain

DESIGNER: ROBERT COMSTOCK - BOISE, ID
BUILDER: W.R. GANN - BOISE, ID

creates a passage from the Mediterranean theme to that of a New York loft. This was accomplished with the use of a railing that gives way

to mottled lath and plaster wall as one climbs the stairs to a surprising indoor garden area. The garden was specially created by the designer (who planned the house as a residence for his mother) to bring his mother's fondness for gardening indoors. The matching brick flooring carries out the outdoor patio garden theme.

The details in the house are all natural in feel from the old-style lath and plaster walls to the three types of maple—including a winter-cut maple used for its different hue—to the walls finished with a buttery-velvet texture.

Chelonia

S U N   V A L L E Y ,   I D A H O

Photography by Alan Weintraub

Chelonia, designed by architect Bart Prince, is nestled on 12 acres in a valley of the mighty Sawtooths near Sun Valley. The shingled roof curves gracefully over the split-faced, honey-colored concrete, which mirrors the texture and flow of the foothills. The complex and organic exterior is held in contrast to the simple interior design. Flowing walls create pockets of space rather than formal rooms within the 3,000-square-foot home. The nucleus is the living room with a massive skylight that arches over the spacious room, bathing it in sunlight. Wings on either side of the main quarters contain the master bedroom and guest rooms. These rooms are markedly different with a warm and comforting ambiance created by the concrete walls. The main level of the home includes a dining area, formal living area with fireplace and entertainment area with built-in bronze cabinetry. The powder room and laundry

ARCHITECT: BART PRINCE - ALBEQUERQUE, NM
BUILDER: JACK MCNAMARA - SUN VALLEY, ID

room, at opposite ends of the great room, are cylindrical in shape and capped by skylights with steel points, framing the view of the sky. The bedrooms are on a slightly lower level, connected by tubular ramp hallways. The master bedroom has two decks with one off the master bath, which includes a Jacuzzi tub. The guest bedroom wing has two bedrooms—each with its own covered deck— and a bath. A large entertainment deck with a Jacuzzi and magnificent views completes the southeast side of the home.

The interior of this home challenges conventional floorplans with its arching ceilings, twisting corridors and curving walls. It is the epitome of organic structure in its ability to both challenge and blend with the landscape.

The home designed by Bart Prince beneath the Sawtooths successfully highlights the contours, textures, and flow of the magnificent landscape. The home is situated on 12 acres at the intersection of three valleys. There is a creek on the north side of the home and the grounds are covered with native grasses, wildflowers, and sagebrush.

The Drackett House

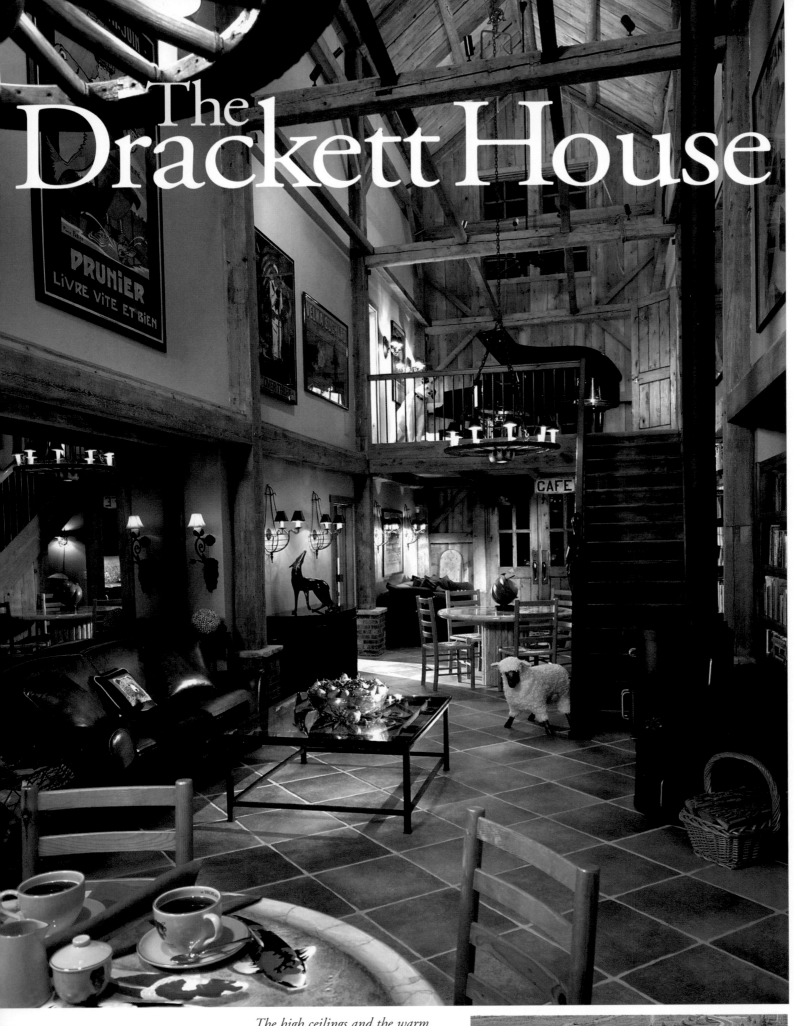

The high ceilings and the warm tones of the decor create an inviting atmosphere at the Drackett House.

Barns supplied by The Barn People - Woodstock, Vermont.

160

KETCHUM, IDAHO
Photography by Kevin Syms

This unique home in the Wood River Valley is constructed of five, 200-year-old Vermont barns, which were dismantled and relocated to the Sun Valley area, making it the oldest building in Idaho. The entrance of the Drackett Barns features a heavy alder door that passes into a sunny gallery hallway. To the right is the living room complete with a European fireplace, flanked by floor-to-ceiling bookshelves. The room's warm feel is created with the cinnamon-colored barn-board ceiling that is supported by hand-hewn white oak beams. Beyond the living room is the master suite accented with oversized furniture and wonderful views through the well-placed windows. A children's hall, formerly a dairy barn, includes four rooms that surround a dramatic common room. The kitchen and dining room feature trusses salvaged from an antique barn in Canada. The countertops are Baltic brown granite and the round dining table easily seats ten. The garage, which has an upstairs office and also serves as a covered walkway to the Orwell Barn with separate living quarters, was a four-bay livery stable.

ARCHITECT: DAMIAN FERRELL GROUP - ANN ARBOR, MI
BUILDER: JACK MCNAMARA - KETCHUM, ID

The House at
Eagle Creek
"Form Follows Landscape"

The House at
Eagle Creek

Opposite page: The copper clad glass pyramids create a striking silhouette on the approach to the residence. At left: The birch walls and ceilings in the living, dining and kitchen areas maximize the effects of light.

KETCHUM, IDAHO

Photography by Tim Brown & Fred Lindholm

This geometrically complex home on Eagle Creek Road north of Ketchum is an unusual creation among the sagebrush hills. The architect's objective was to lift the human spirit, and the expression of that desire is most notable in the five plaster and glass-capped pyramids that rise up from the rooftop. From the exterior, the pyramids create their own ridge of mountaintops, which is suited to the geography of the Eagle Creek area. The glass tops create a wonderful experience of light and reflection once inside. Each pyramid rises out of a different section of the home, giving the sense of a ceiling plan rather than floor plan. The largest pyramid rises over the living area, and the nearest two shed light on the dining and kitchen areas. The fourth and fifth provide a lighted intimacy to bedrooms.

ARCHITECT : JACK SMITH, FAIA - KETCHUM, ID
BUILDER : INTERMOUNTAIN CONSTRUCTION - IDAHO FALLS, ID - JEFF OGDEN

*M*ultiple views of the house at Eagle Creek demonstrate how it re-interprets the landscape to become its own mountain reflection.

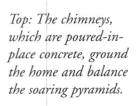

Top: The chimneys, which are poured-in-place concrete, ground the home and balance the soaring pyramids.

KETCHUM, IDAHO

The Ellis House

The Ellis House is a chic modernist home situated on the aspen and spruce tree acreage of Golden Eagle Ranch in the Sun Valley area. The main vista for the home is the historic Union Pacific Railway Bridge, an arched trussed creation that spans the Big Wood River and inspired the design of the Ellis home. The architect incorporated the trussed bridge curvature by including a thirty-six-foot-long, sky lit Porte-Cochere colonnade entrance. The cantilevered canopy leads visitors to the dramatic five-foot-wide pivotal rusted steel entry door. The floor-to-ceiling windows in the living room create a frame for the historic bridge view. Visible from the entryway is a double helix staircase, and a circular powder room with an elevated glass sink mounted on a curly maple sculptured pedestal. The grandiose round dining room opens in to the kitchen with ample storage in stainless steel floor-to-ceiling pull out cabinets.

ARCHITECT: EDDY SVIDGAL - KETCHUM, ID
BUILDER: FRANK BASHISTA - KETCHUM, ID

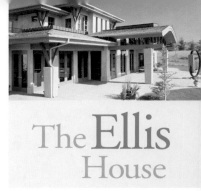

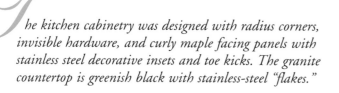

The kitchen cabinetry was designed with radius corners, invisible hardware, and curly maple facing panels with stainless steel decorative insets and toe kicks. The granite countertop is greenish black with stainless-steel "flakes."

The interior fabrics, carpets, and colors are predominately soft to deep golds and purples contrasted with light woods, steel, glass, aluminum and concrete. The overall effect combines a modern edginess against the color schemes of the mountainous region.

MONTANA *MONTANA* *MONTANA* *MONTANA* *MONTANA* *MONTANA* *MONTANA* *MONTANA* *MONTANA* *MONTANA* MC

A collection of Montana's most original and distinctive homes.

MONTANA

Soaring Osprey House, Beattie Residence, Duck Shack

*M*ontana provides the world with some of the most majestic mountain scenes found in the Pacific Northwest. It is one of the few states left that truly represents the unspoiled natural beauty it was blessed with. Montana is an area that provides a peaceful serenity to all who experience its wonderment.

Amidst the spectacular mountains, shimmering lakes and productive ranch land, there lies a wonderful lifestyle, a sportsman's paradise, and the setting for some of the most awe inspiring homes one can imagine. Some of these very impressive homes are presented in this section for your reading enjoyment.

The Soaring Osprey House

FLATHEAD LAKE, MONTANA

Photography by Roger Wade

This unique home is perched on rugged land overlooking the bay on Montana's Flathead Lake in the Rocky Mountains. A 30-mile view down the lake presents some breathtaking scenery and a fantastic opportunity to observe the natural wildlife of the area. The home's design was inspired by the winged flight of eagles and osprey hawks that frequent the lake. The curved roofline resembles wings, while the two-tone roof tiles were used to simulate birds' feathers. The shape of the impressive 30' foot high steel reinforced curved windows was designed to give the impression of feathered wings.

ARCHITECT: RICHARD WYMAN SMITH – WHITEFISH, MT
BUILDER: FORD CONSTRUCTION – KALISPELL, MT
INTERIOR DESIGNERS: CAROL LARKIN – HAMILTON, MT,
CAROL NELSON – KALISPELL, MT
CHERYL McGILL – SAN DIEGO, CA

The interior lines are kept clean and simple to avoid contrasting with the massive windows. The maple flooring and the wrought iron balcony supports, designed to suggest gently blowing lake reeds, further enhance the natural harmony of the space. During the construction of this 7,000 square foot structure, the environment was allowed to dictate the style, creating a home that is one with its surroundings.

Once inside, a person is immediately involved with the outside. And while the exterior views are intoxicating, the rounded ceiling and walls create an atmosphere of warmth and security that promotes a very calming effect on the inhabitants. The total experience is both exciting and serene.

Spread information source: Montana Living Magazine, Winter of 1999, and Cowboys and Indians Magazine, 1996.

The
Beattie Residence

Photography by Roger Wade

Located in the Madison River Valley of Southwestern Montana, this rustic beauty has been created from three log barns built in 1890. All of the stones used throughout the home are the tailings from an old gold mine located on the property.

The home uses materials from the natural surroundings and the craftsmanship of local artists to create unique features such as a moose antler chandelier, a wood and stone entryway, and a western style porch.

ARCHITECT: CANDACE TILLOTSON MILLER –
  LIVINGSTON, MT
BUILDER: YELLOWSTONE TRADITIONS – BOZEMAN, MT
INTERIOR DESIGNER: DIANE BEATTIE – ENNIS, MT

In creating her ideal cabin, the owner looked to national parks, the Adirondacks and the Black Forest for inspiration. Tall windows allow natural light to bathe the interior. Sofas and club chairs are upholstered with glove leather laced with rawhide and Texas cowhide to help maintain a warm and cozy living space.

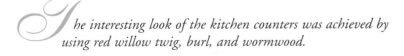 he interesting look of the kitchen counters was achieved by using red willow twig, burl, and wormwood.

A fireplace on the exterior patio provides a wonderful ambiance on cold winter days.

The focal points of the master bedroom are the natural stone fireplace and four-poster bed, dressed with a Pierre Deux quilt and a French throw. Tea-washed kilims and kazaks provide a warmth of color.

The Duck Shack

Photography by Roger Wade

*I*f Frank Lloyd Wright had ever decided to build a duck blind, this is what it would look like. When owner/architect Jack Gordon decided to replace his father's traditional, but ailing, duck blind, he ended up creating something both the hunters and the ducks were not quite sure about. However, the American Institute of Architects certainly was sure, and awarded him the 1996 Montana Design Award for his wonderful creation.

The Duck Shack was literally designed around the windows, a style right out of the 1900-1910 Wright period. Their design set the tone for the other materials and colors, right down to the steel base that provides the strength necessary to allow the windows to completely encircle the structure. Cherokee red windows dictated cherry cabinets and jet-black marble countertops as the proper accents.

ARCHITECT, BUILDER, INTERIOR DESIGNER:
GORDON CONSTRUCTION – FLATHEAD LAKE, MT

$\mathcal{T}$he cantilevered decks were designed to maximize an unobstructed view and can support 67 people with hunting apparatus, or cocktails, as the circumstances dictate. The end result is the most beautifully appointed "duck blind" that one is ever likely to see.

One would think the ducks hardly stand a chance with all that caviar and those attractive color schemes, but Jack admits that the abode's functions have given way primarily to social events and some occasional skeet shooting these days.

Spread information source:
Big Sky Journal Magazine, 1997

British

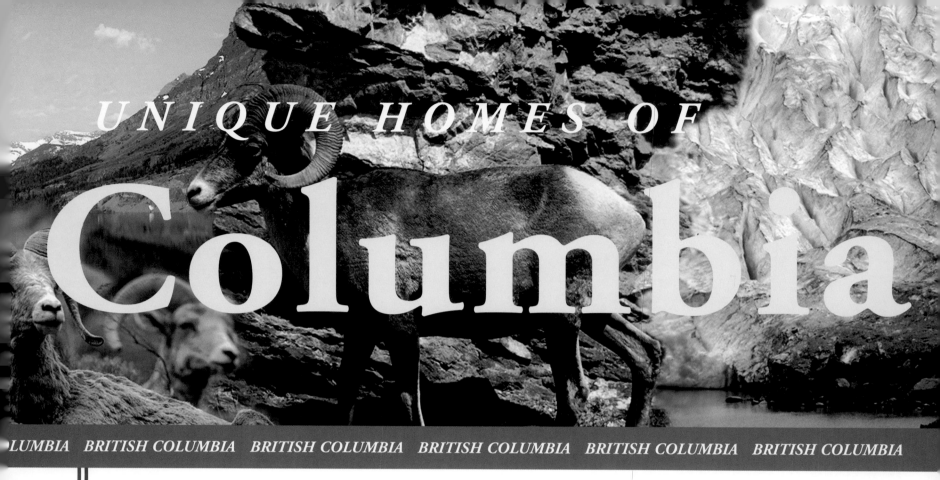

UNIQUE HOMES OF
Columbia

A collection of British Columbia's most original and distinctive homes.

BRITISH COLUMBIA

The Argo, Splendor on Lake Okanagan, Thornhill Home, Mushroom House, Bosa Residence

Western Canada has the very best the world has to offer: endless mountain wilderness and pristine lakes for the nature enthusiast, world-class skiing at destinations like Banff and Whistler, and plenty of coastal waterways for the nautically inclined. British Columbia also encompasses one of the largest metropolitan areas in North America, with excellent shopping and a wide range of cultural diversity in the Vancouver area.

Within this Pacific Northwest wonderland exists some of the most unique homes that can be found anywhere. This section provides you with an up-close and personal look into some of these beautiful homes.

The Argo House

This unique mountain retreat evolved from the owners' initial concept of a vessel into a wonderfully creative home. The home's namesake, the Argo, is from the mythological ship of Jason and the Argonauts. Many of the designs used throughout the house maintain this theme to create a "psycho-physical" effect, wherein the home seems to be a structure that both transports and contains. The entire home manifests the owners' philosophy of "the inter-connectedness of all things".

Photography by Alec Pyt' low' a' ny/© and
Greg Eymundson/Insight Photography International

ARCHITECT: BRIAN HEMINGWAY ARCHITECT LTD. –
  WEST VANCOUVER, B.C.
BUILDER: WHIRLWIND HOMES LTD. - WHISTLER, B.C.

*A*ll doors and millwork are custom made and designed, while wide-planked European beech and green slate from Pakistan form all of the floors. Stone figured prominently, as seen in Brazilian granite kitchen counters, German limestone fireplaces, and bathroom counters. Suspended panels of sandblasted glass accentuate ceilings.

The centering piece of the residence is the fireplace, a stunning glass and stone work of art called "Spirits of the Pacific Northwest" created by artist Susan Point.

The exterior of the home is cedar and copper, with diamond-shaped copper tiles on some vertical surfaces emulating a wavelike effect.

The tranquil waterfall at the entrance, basalt stone walls, and the wilderness environment add to the serene qualities of this wonderful Whistler hide-a-way.

Splendor on
Lake Okanagan

KELOWNA, BRITISH COLUMBIA

Photography by Michael Mathers

This starkly beautiful white house sits on the banks of Lake Okanagan below 40 acres of vineyards on the award winning Cedar Creek Winery in Kelowna, B.C. The home encompasses wonderful wide-open spaces with uninterrupted views of the lake, vineyards and surrounding landscape.

ARCHITECT: DEMETRIOU ARCHITECTS – KIRKLAND, WA
INTERIOR DESIGNER: RICHARD SALTER INTERIORS – VANCOUVER, B.C.

Senator Ross Fitzpatrick and his wife Linda have a fondness for American Indian art, especially Navaho artifacts. A mixture of items from France, Italy, and China, as well as several Andy Warhol paintings, create a subtle and pleasant cross-cultural ambiance.

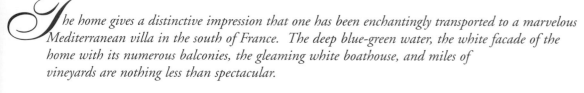

The home gives a distinctive impression that one has been enchantingly transported to a marvelous Mediterranean villa in the south of France. The deep blue-green water, the white facade of the home with its numerous balconies, the gleaming white boathouse, and miles of vineyards are nothing less than spectacular.

The pool and deck area presents stupendous views of the lake and surrounding areas. The boat house plays a key role in the home's style and adds to the family's ability to enjoy beautiful Lake Okanagan.

Spread information source:
Author, Brad Ovenenell-Carter,
"The Grapes of Ross", Aug. 1992

WHISTLER, BRITISH COLUMBIA

*Photography by Greg Eymundson/
Insight Photography International*

This beautiful home is perched high above Alpha Lake in a position that takes full advantage of the water views and of majestic Whistler Mountain. This residence is the ultimate entertaining home with large open spaces designed to make each area feel surprisingly intimate. Clever use of different levels and ceiling heights ranging from 9 to 40 feet create unique rooms that make the home ideal for personal use and large group gatherings.

The home could be described as a Whistler Tuscan. The floors on the main floor are Pennsylvanian blue stone, radiantly heated for the added comfort of those who prefer to go shoeless. The massive Tuscan fireplace burns brightly most of the year and helps enhance the comfortable feeling imparted throughout the home.

ARCHITECT: DENNIS MAGUIRE – WHISTLER, B.C.
BUILDER: BENBOW CONSTRUCTION – WHISTLER, B.C.
INTERIOR DESIGNERS:
  TRICIA GUIGUET DESIGNS – WHISTLER, B.C.
  INTRINSIC DESIGNS – WEST VANCOUVER, B.C.

Custom milled logs give the structure a sturdy, handcrafted feeling and fit perfectly with the rugged terrain of Whistler.

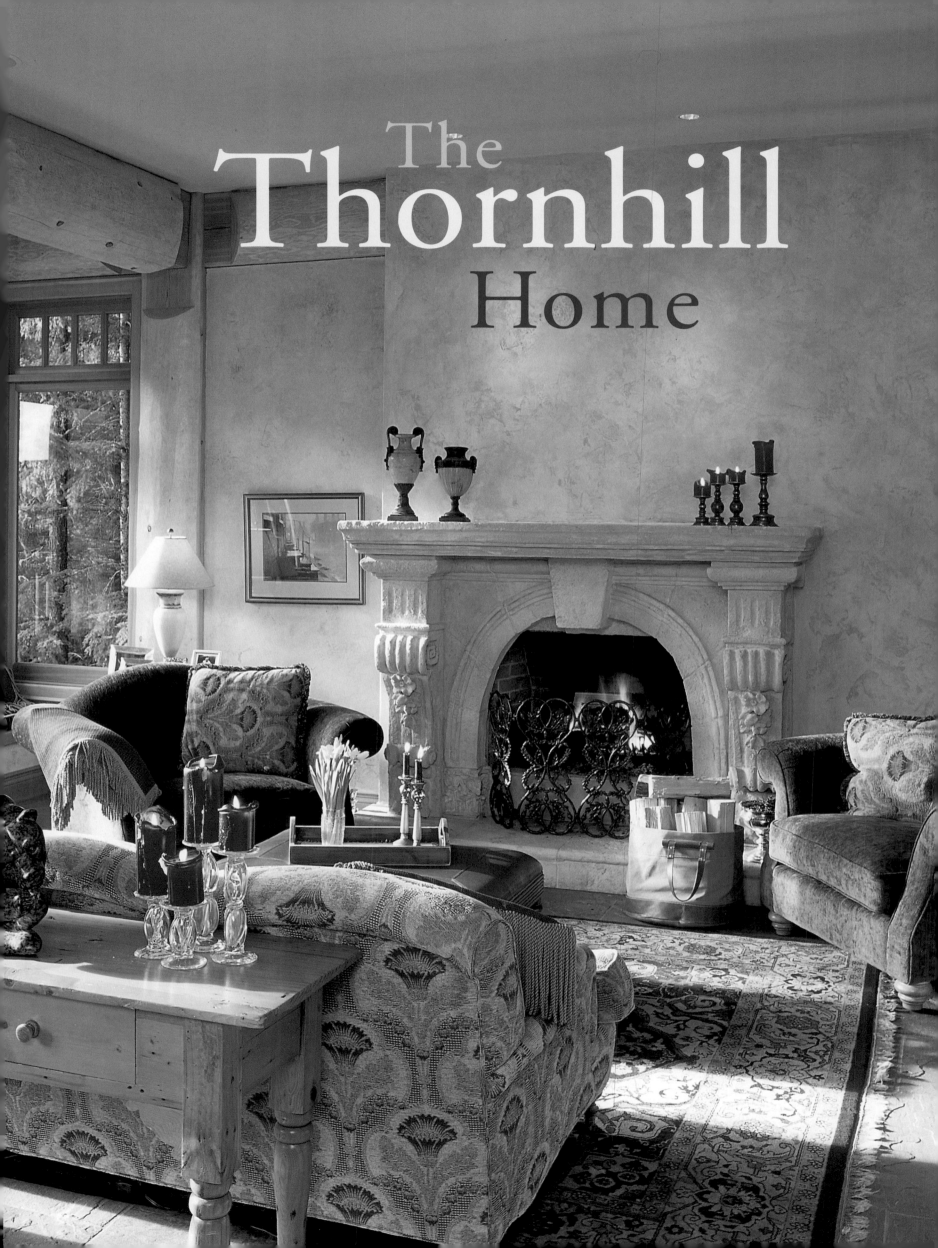

The Thornhill Home

*T*he kitchen has a strong European flavor. The use of travertine, large carved finials, French plumbing fixtures, and an English farmhouse sink adds to the flare. It opens into the spacious dining and living areas to provide the ideal environment for enjoyment by all.

The lower level of the home is strictly for entertainment. The media room is reminiscent of Out of Africa, while the games room has a full size pool table and double doors leading out to a large hot tub deck, complete with steam shower.

The gorgeous master bedroom suite is set apart from the other areas of the house to maintain privacy. Children's bedrooms have their own area, complete with private baths and sun-decks, while guests have their own private wing, with two bedrooms, adjoining baths, and a living area with all the facilities and comforts of home.

The Mushroom House

Photography by Greg Eymundson/Insight Photography International

*T*his Tolkenian-like masterpiece epitomizes the definition of a "unique home." Perfectly situated in a mountain setting near Whistler in British Columbia, this home is a hand-crafted labor of love that truly defines its architect owner.

From the basement pool and sauna, to the hand-laid ceramic tile floor on the main level and the mushroom-shaped roof and overhangs, the artistry expresses true individualism in every square inch of this fantastic home.

ARCHITECT & BUILDER: ZUBE ALYWARD – WHISTLER, B.C.

The home seems to wrap around a monumentally impressive fireplace made from natural local materials and creates a magical environment that gives the impression you have somehow passed over a mysterious threshold into an entirely different world filled with magical beings from another time and place.

It is virtually impossible to walk anywhere in the home without being amazed at the handiwork, time, and effort that created this architectural marvel. The original construction took twelve years to complete, then another ten years to rebuild after a serious fire occurred. Every rock, stone and piece of wood has the personal touch of the artist, right down to the furniture, stairways and banisters, dragon carving, window frames, cabinets and countertops.

The
Bosa
Residence

Photography by Greg Eymundson/Insight Photography International

This fantastic home is secluded far at the end of the road, suspended high above a golf course, overlooking a magnificence view of Whistler Mountain. The home has a wonderful openness, centered around the fireplace that is embraced by massive logs rising to the octagonal shaped skylight in the roof high above. The skylight reflects the form of a snow flake on the surfaces below and provides a great deal of natural light to the area.

Everything in the kitchen is imported from Germany, including the sinks, appliances, countertops, and cabinets, right down to the unique hinges and the cherry wood used in the wine storage area. The master bed room has a very elegant feel with its high domed ceiling supported by cherry beams, a granite fireplace, central African antique headpiece, and breathtaking views.

ARCHITECT: KLAUS BUDDE – VANCOUVER, B.C.
BUILDER: BOSA CONSTRUCTION – BURNABY, B.C.
INTERIOR DESIGNER: PAOLA GARM – VANCOUVER, B.C.

The outside areas of the home takes full advantage of Whistler's mesmerizing scenery. Outdoor walkways connect the pool, spa, and sun decks to the main house. Beyond the golf course and wooded area, one has a perfect view of the Blackcomb ski runs on Whistler Mountain.

The wonderful combination of granite, marble, and stone, combined with the natural wood beams and timbers throughout the house, give the home a sense that is best described as "mountain elegance". Much of the granite used in the home is a rare Italian granite from the Sarpegna Islands and is among the last made available before the quarry closed recently. The granite has a burnt finish that softens the marble to allow it to sparkle when the sun shines on it, but creates a very warm and powdery, matte finish in more subdued light.

Craftsmen
& Designer Credits

The Villa at John's Peak

ARCHITECTS:
Michael Helm Architects, Ltd.
Tortola, British Virgin Islands

Bruce Richey
Bruce Richey Architect, AIA
1941 Westerlund Drive
Medford, Oregon 97501
(541) 773-4025
bwrichey@internetcds.com
www.oregonarchitect.com

BUILDERS: Richard Krebs & Bruce Gledhill
Hartsook Construction
332 S. Front Street, Medford, OR 97501
(541) 773-5987   hartsookconst.com
www.hartsookconstruction@cs.com

Double River Ranch

BUILDER:
Yellowstone Traditions
P.O. Box 1933
Bozeman, MT 59771
(406) 587-0968
cderham@yellowstonetraditions.com

The Beattie Residence

ARCHITECT: Jon R. Sayler, AIA. PS.
204 S. Koren Rd. Ste 700
Spokane Vally, WA 99212
(509) 535-9207   saylerjr@qwest.net
INTERIOR DESIGNER: Debbie Shaffer
DGS Interiors, 223 N. Bellevue Avenue
Walla Walla, WA 99362
(509) 522-9419

ARCHITECT:
Kirkland Cutter
BUILDER/REMODELER:
Pat Jeppesen Construction
1016 W. Railroad Avenue
Spokane, WA   99201
(509) 624-9383

The Brett Residence

The House at Eagle Bluff

BUILDER:
Oceanco/2002
Guildo Pastor Centre
7 Rue de Gabian
MC9800, Monaco
+37 7 93 10 02 80
INTERIOR DESIGNER:
Franco Zuretti
Zuretti Interior Designers

Lady Lola Yacht

ARCHITECT: Jon R. Sayler, AIA. PS.
204 S. Koren Rd. Ste 700
Spokane Vally, WA 99212
(509) 535-9207   saylerjr@qwest.net
BUILDER: Dan Olson
Daniel J. Olson Construction, Inc.
P.O. Box 13246
Spokane, WA 99213
(509) 928-9209   dan@gntech.net
INTERIOR DESIGNER: Mara Newlun
R. Alan Brown, Inc.
E. 10303 Sprague
Spokane, WA 99206
(509) 924-7200 or (509) 991-5498

ARCHITECT & BUILDER: Tom Kelly
Neil Kelly Designers/Remodeler
804 N. Alberta
Portland, OR 97217
(503) 288-7461
www.neilkelly.com

Snyder's Snug Harbor

Publisher:
Rhinobooks
www.rhinobooks.net

In Harmony With Puget Sound

BUILDER: Donna Shirey CGR, CAPS
Shirey Contracting Incorporation
230 NE Juniper Street
Issaquah, WA 98027
(425) 427-1300
donna@shireycontracting.com
www.shireycontracting.com

Elk Rock Road Residence

Livable Art at Pike's Peak

BUILDER: Terry Thompson
Thompson Residential Development
2812 120th Avenue NE
Bellevue, WA 98005
(425) 466-8491   terrya2@mindspring.com
INTERIOR DESIGNER: Sally Thompson
Sally's Interior Design
Bellevue, WA 98005
(425) 702-9215   terrya2@mindspring.com

ARCHITECT: Robert H. Oshatz
12560 SW Elk Rock Road
Lake Oswego, OR 97034
(503) 635-4243   robert@oshatz.com
www.oshatz.com

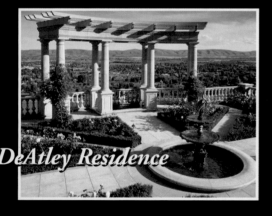

DeAtley Residence

ARCHITECT & INTERIOR ARCHITECTURE:
Vassos M. Demetriou
Demetriou Architects
5555 Lakeview Dr., Suite 200
Kirkland, WA 98003
(425) 827-1700   VMD@demetriou.net
www.demetriouarchitects.com
INTERIOR DESIGNER:
Edward Maske & Joe Simon
Shopkeeper
3105 Summitview Avenue
Yakima, WA 98902
(509) 452-6646 or (888) 577-2356
shopkpr@aol.com - www.shopkpr.com

First Hill Living in Seattle

ARCHITECT: Norman Sandler
Sandler Kilburn Architects, LLC
1661 E. Olive Way, Suite 200
Seattle, WA 98102
(206) 682-5211
www.sandlerarchitects.com
BUILDER: Denny Howell
Shawnee Construction, LLC
2613 Meadow Avenue N
Renton, WA 98056   (425) 226- 0
denny@shawneeconstructionllc.com
www.shawneeconstructionllc.com
INTERIOR DESIGNER: Elisabeth Beers
Sandler Kilburn Architects, LLC
1661 E. Olive Way, Suite 200
Seattle, WA 98102
(206) 682-5211
elisabeth@sandlerarchitects.com

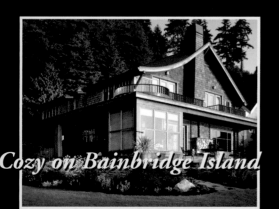

Cozy on Bainbridge Island

ARCHITECT & INTERIOR DESIGNERS:
Peter Brachvogel, AIA
BC&J Architects PS
197 Parfitt Way SW, Suite 120
Bainbridge Isl, WA 98110
(206) 780-9113
peterb@bcandj.com   www.bcandj.com
BUILDER:
Bill Corbin
W.M. Corbin Const. Corp.
8719 Battle Point Rd. NE
Bainbridge Isl, WA 98110
(206) 842-5538   buildcorbin@yahoo.com

Serene Retreat

ARCHITECT:
Neal Huston Architect, AIA
19795 Village Office Court
Bend, OR 97702
(541) 389-0991
info@nealhuston.com
www.nealhuston.com
BUILDER/RESTORATION
Ed Adams
Handcrafted Log Homes
P.O. Box 625
Sisters, OR 97759
(541) 815-4602

At Home on the Ranch

ARCHITECT: Saul Zaik, F.A.I.A.
Zaik/Miller Associates
Architects/Planners
2340 NW Thurman, Ste. 201
Portland, OR 97210
(503) 222-9158
BUILDER:
Barnard & Kinney
Portland, OR

BUILDER: Bob Barden
Barden Construction Co.
6939 SW GalleySt.
Lincoln City, OR 97367
(541) 996-2794
bbarden@charter.net

Mollie B-By the Sea

Pigeon Point Beach House

DESIGNER: Tom Kelly
Neil Kelly Designers/Remodelers
804 N. Alberta
Portland, OR 97217
(503) 288-7461
www.neilkelly.com

Twin Points Peninsula

ARCHITECT:
Obie G. Bowman Architect, AIA
P.O. Box 1114
Healdsburg, CA 95448
(707) 433-7833   ogb@sonic.net
BUILDER:
John Harper
Nomad Designs
32120 N. Chantrelle Lane
Gold Beach, OR 97444
(541) 247-0351   waves@wave.net

ARCHITECT & BUILDER:
Dennis Batke
Dennis Batke Architecture AIA, RIBA
1810 N.W. Overton
Portland, OR 97209
(503) 242-9391
dennis@dbarchitecture.com
INTERIOR DESIGNER:
Karol Niemi
Karol Niemi Associates
1810 N.W. Overton
Portland, OR 97209
(503) 222-3426

Batke-Niemi Residence

Publisher:
Rhinobooks, LLC
www.rhinobooks.net

belonia

ARCHITECT: Bart Prince
3501 Monte Vista NE
Albuquerque, NM 87106
(505) 256-1961
BUILDER:
Jack McNamara
Ketchum, ID
(208) 726-2372

Hetland House

bie Springs

ARCHITECT:
Arthur Dennis Stevens, AIA
Architectural Enterprises, LTD
111 Broadway, Suite 133-179
Boise, ID 83702
(208) 426-8199   www.robiesprings.com

BUILDER:
J Bar K & Associates
209 South Eagle Rd.
Eagle, ID 83616
(208) 939-8800

e Healy Tree House

DESIGN & INTERIOR DESIGN:
Deanne Healy
Healy Interior Design and Space Planning
P.O. Box 514
Sandpoint, ID 83864
(208) 263-8728
jimhealy@leadlok.com

Eagle's Perch

ARCHITECT: BRS Architects
1010 S. Allante Place, Suite 100
Boise, ID 83709
(208) 336-8370
BUILDER: Randy Hemmer
Randy Hemmer Construction, LLC
10552 Garverdale Ct., Suite 908
Boise, ID 83704
(208) 376-0358
rshemmer@aol.com
INTERIOR DESIGN: Barrie Connolly
Barrie Connolly & Associates
2188 Bluestem Lane
Boise, ID 83706
(208) 345-6225

agadone House

ARCHITECT & DESIGNER:
Warren Sheets Design
195 Erie Street
San Francisco, CA 94109
(415) 626-2320

Comstock

ARCHITECT: Eddy Svidgal
P.O. Box 4750
Ketchum, ID 83340
(208) 726-1014

Ellis House

ARCHITECT & INTERIOR DESIGN:
Beverly McGuire
Robert Comstock
P.O. Box 2898
Boise, ID 83702-2898
(208) 363-9000
beverly.mcguire@robertcomstock.com

ARCHITECT: Jack Smith, FAIA
Smith & Associates, PA
P.O. Box 3000
Ketchum, ID 83340
(208) 726-3400   jsfaia@sunvalley.com
BUILDER: Jeff Ogden, President
Intermountain Construction, Inc.
P.O. Box 2319
Idaho Falls, ID 83403
(208) 524-4322
holly_peterson@interconst.com

Eagle Creek

Drackett House

DESIGNER: Glen Cloninger, AIA
Glen A. Cloninger & Associates
104 S. Freya Street, Suite 209D
Spokane, WA 99202
(509) 535-3619   cloningerarch@aol.com

Cloninger House

ARCHITECT:
Damion Ferell Group
Los Angeles, CA
BUILDER:
Jack McNamara
Ketchum, ID
(208) 726-2372

ARCHITECT: Richard W. Smith
Richard Wyman Smith Architect
P.O. Box 1558
Whitefish, MT 59937
(406) 862-7883   indigo@digisys.net
INTERIOR DESIGNER: Carol Nelson
Carol Nelson Design
423 1st Avenue E.
Kalispell, MT 59901
(406) 752-6175   cndesign@nelsondesign.com

The Soaring Osprey House

Publisher:
Rhinobooks, LLC
www.rhinobooks.net

The Argo

ARCHITECT: Brian Hemingway
Brian Hemingway Architect, Ltd.
5220 Keith Road
West Vancouver, B.C. Canada V7W 2N1
(604) 921-1203   hemingwaybrian@shaw.ca

BUILDER: Brad Sills
Whirlwind Homes
P.O. Box 436
Whistler, B.C. Canada V0N 1B2
(604) 932-7779

The Thornhill Home

Splendor on Lake Okanagan

ARCHITECT: Vassos M. Demetriou
Demetriou Architects PLLS
5555 Lakeview Dr., Suite 200
Kirkland, WA 98033
(425) 827-1700   VMD@demetriou.net
www.demetriouarchitects.com

ARCHITECT: Dennis Maguire
Dennis Maguire Architects
9580 Emerald Bay
Whistler, B.C. Canada
(604) 905-7777

BUILDER: John Benbow
Benbow Custom Homes
Box 1340
Whistler, B.C. Canada V0N 1B0
(604) 932-8794

INTERIOR DESIGNERS:
Tricia Guiguet
Tricia Guiguet Interior Design
1064 Millar Creek Road
Whistler, B.C. Canada V0N 1B1
(604)938-4700 tgid@whooshnet.com

Susan Parker
Intrinsic Interiors Design, Inc.
2720 Rosebery Avenue
West Vancouver, B.C. Canada V7V 3A2
(604) 926-2372
susan@intrinsicinteriors.com
www.intrinsicinteriors.com

Bosa Residence

DESIGN & INTERIOR DESIGN:
Klaus Budde
192 W. 23rd Avenue
Vancouver, B.C. Canada V5Y 2G9
(604) 876-3558

BUILDER:
Bosa Construction
1200–4555 Kingsway
Burnaby, B.C. V5H 4T8
(604) 299-1363

INTERIOR DESIGN: Paola Garm
Roche Bobois
716 W. Hastings
Vancouver, B.C. Canada V6C 1A3
(604) 669-5443   info@visavisinteriors.com
www.rochebobois.com